GETTING ST
WITH THE
DAILY OFFICE
IN THE HOUSEHOLD

A PRAYER GUIDE
FOR INDIVIDUALS AND FAMILIES

The
Trinity
Mission

the**trinity**mission.org

ISBN 979-8-9854410-3-1 paperback
ISBN 979-8-9854410-2-4 spiral

A Note About This Edition

Getting Started with the Daily Office in the Household (for Individuals & Families) is a project in process produced by The Trinity Mission. By purchasing this copy, you are helping us to develop helpful resources for Christian formation. Thank you.

———————————

If you would like to give us feedback about this resource or to discover more resources for ancient Christian formation, please visit our website: the**trinity**mission.org.

CONTENTS

GETTING STARTED WITH THE DAILY OFFICE

DISCUSSION, INSTRUCTIONS, AND EXPLANATIONS

(Feel free to skip over the parts you don't need)

This book is a guide for developing the habit of daily prayer. The forms of prayer here are the Western Church's historical services for Morning Prayer, Mid-Day Prayer, Evening Prayer, and Compline. Various traditions have slight differences (Benedictine, Anglican, Lutheran, Roman Catholic, Western Rite Orthodox, etc). The particularities here are drawn from the Anglican/Benedictine/Western Rite tradition and based primarily on the 2019 Book of Common Prayer.

The Daily Offices are rooted in the ancient Christian practice of setting apart certain times of the day for specific prayer and meditation in God's word. You'll find that Christians all over the world and through the ages have prayed almost identically (though in other languages perhaps) to the way you'll be praying with this book.

The text here should be seen as an aid and not an idol. These words are not magic incantations. They are simply the very words of God or that which is clearly based on Scripture. It is good to pray just as the text leads you to pray, however, for some of you, that may seem very formal or "inauthentic"… read on!

WHY CALL IT AN "OFFICE"

That does seem to be an odd word doesn't it? These prayers are also called the Divine Office, the Divine Services, and the Liturgy of the Hours – this last one because they serve to mark times of the day. Later, we will discuss briefly the history of the Daily Office (for those who are interested in such things) but for now, I think it is helpful to make the following observations:

I came from a modern tradition that looked poorly upon formal prayer. Knowing that prayer was "talking to God," "pouring out my heart to God," "interceding with God" – all very true things – I felt that prayer should primarily be about authentically telling God what I am thinking or feeling. There is absolutely nothing wrong with that… but it's not likely going to change me.

Besides, God already knows those things. I'm not telling Him anything new. On top of that, I may not be thinking or feeling very holy right now, so perhaps it might not be such a good idea to dwell on what I'm thinking or feeling at this moment.

When learning about the Daily Office, I kept being confronted with the ideas that it is a "work" to be done, an "activity," an "offering." In many ways, it is an *exercise*. If I want tight abs, I'm not going to get them by talking about how much I want to start exercising or sharing my feelings about health and wellness. I'm going to have to *do* something.

But I can't make myself holy, not even one inch more. I've discovered that a million or so times to be true.

Think about this analogy: my family enjoys birds. Let's say that, for some reason, we wanted to fill our house with songbirds (the Holy Spirit of Christ). Clearly, just hoping for songbirds won't do much. Also, encouraging cats in our yard and cutting down all the trees and uprooting the shrubs would work against our goal.

So, we might set out on a "work" of planting trees and bushes, setting out feeders and water sources. Then, of most importance, we would have to actually open our windows and doors and create an interior space that was hospitable to songbirds.

Having done all that, in the end, we have no control over whether the songbirds will actually come in or not. What the songbirds do is their business. Creating a home for them is ours.

That is what the Daily Office does. It is a changing of *our* heart and mind, a surrendering of our will. It is communion with God by saying "yes

Lord," and "speak Lord, for your servant is listening." It is saying things that I may NOT actually be thinking and/or feeling with the desire that I want to be thinking or feeling those things.

In the Office I do the work, the effort, the activity of creating a home for Christ in myself and in my household. It is my (re-) offering of my self to God throughout the day.

SO, HOW MANY OF THE SERVICES DO I NEED TO DO

That depends on you and your life situation. You're not a monk. They pray these things up to eight times a day. Chances are, though, that you have a job and/or family and other obligations to attend to.

In the history section later, we will talk about what Christians have done in the past. For now, I recommend working toward doing something in the morning, something in the evening, and a brief pause of recollection in the middle of the day and before bed. But start with just one of these, probably Morning Prayer.

DO I NEED TO DO THE WHOLE THING

Briefly: no.

The basic form of the Office is this: the Opening Dialogue, Scripture reading (psalms mostly), the Lord's Prayer and other prayers. I generally suggest that people work toward doing the full Morning Office as their private (i.e. alone) morning prayer time.

After that, it highly depends on your life situation.

If you have the time, it is always advisable to do the full office at other times of the day as well. But if not, perhaps you can add in a brief recollection at mid-day (p. 200), evening (p. 202), and bed-time (p. 204) as your standard daily schedule.

For families, I suggest coming up with something to do together at least once a day. It doesn't matter which office you pick. Choose according to your family schedule. You may want to start with the General Structure for Family Prayer (see p. 205) and add into it the elements that are appropriate for your family's age and time constraints.

It is also advisable to have at least one time a week where you do a full Office with a group. This could be a good time to invite others over to join you or to start something with your local church.

An additional note: if you are thinking, "if I say Morning Prayer by myself can I still do Morning Prayer with my family or church." Answer: absolutely. You may want to find different Scripture reading plans for each but even that is not necessary. You will enjoy both times differently.

Another note: this book contains a simplified version of the Office for home use. You can always add more parts in later as you get comfortable with the form.

WHO READS WHAT PARTS

In a family or a small group, one person should be the Officiant and everyone (including the Officiant) should say those things marked for "All." You may want to designate one or two people to read the Scripture Lessons instead of the Officiant. This is a really good time to get the children involved with leading the family by reading a part of the prayer time.

If you are reading as an individual, you should read all the parts and you should do so aloud if you can (at least a whisper). Additionally, you may choose to make pronouns singular rather than plural (i.e. "We" becomes "I") although many people prefer to leave them plural to remind themselves that Christians do not pray alone but rather as the Body of Christ.

Whether you are reading as an individual or a family / small group, you may want to join The Trinity Mission online for a while to get a feeling for how it flows. You can do that at the**trinity**mission.org or via iTunes.

WHEN TO DO WHICH SERVICE

Morning Prayer ideally is said in the morning of course. Mid-day sometime around lunch time. Evening Prayer just before supper. And Compline sometime after supper – usually just before bed time.

If you are trying to establish a family evening time routine, either the service for Evening Prayer or for Compline may be used. Evening Prayer has more variety in Scripture readings if you use a lectionary. Compline is intended for use at the time before going to bed and can be more quickly memorized.

WHERE SHOULD WE PRAY

Prayer can be done anywhere. You may find yourself whispering Mid-Day Prayer at your desk during lunch hour or sitting on a park bench. A husband and wife may have Morning Prayer together sitting on the couch in the living room. A family might do Evening Prayer at the dinner table.

If you have space, you may want to make a "prayer corner" with a picture of Jesus, a cross, and some candles. The smallest efforts of making a particular and special place for prayer can help so much in focusing your attention on the Lord and offering yourself to Him.

HOW LONG WILL IT TAKE

If you join us at the**trinity**mission.org, you'll find that our podcast services take from about 8 minutes (at Mid-day Prayer) to 15 minutes (at Morning Prayer). Some days you may find that our speed on the podcast is too fast and that you'd rather spend more time reflecting upon a reading or listening in silence. Other days, you may feel that you're too pressed for time to do the whole thing.

Recognizing that doing the whole liturgy is good and is the most beneficial toward growth in Christ, you will over time have to figure out how things work for you and your life.

It is good for us to establish the rhythm of our lives according to prayer and communion with our Lord and NOT according to the busyness of our schedules. So, remember - on the one hand, we need to be concerned that the schedule of things we have deemed *urgent* does not overcome that which is *important* in our lives. In other words, don't let your busy-ness run your life.

On the other hand, we should be careful that what is "ideal" in terms of form and time does not become the enemy of that which can still be excellent (i.e. it is better to pray only the psalm than to do nothing at all).

All that to say, during times of increased activity in your life, it is totally OK to do less than the full office even if you usually only do one full office a day. That is why we offer the shorter versions that we call "recollections" (pp. 198-204) But at the same time, don't let your busyness keep you from developing a fuller prayer life.

HOW SHOULD WE SIT (OR DO WE STAND? OH WAIT.... KNEEL?)

If you are bold enough, you might try to stand as you pray - even with your hands open upwards in the traditional, Christian posture of prayer. Or you could kneel. The position of your body is <u>not</u> unimportant, for we are after all physical creatures... more on this in a moment.

Although it is perfectly acceptable to sit, it is usually the practice to display some form of reverence whenever The Holy Trinity is mentioned. You may simply make the sign of the Cross over yourself. However, in the West, this reverence has usually been shown by bowing.

So, for instance, if you were in a formal service at a western church or monastery it might look like this:

{Sitting}
Psalm 134

Behold, bless the LORD, all you servants of the LORD,
who stand by night in the house of the LORD!

Lift up your hands in the sanctuary,
and bless the LORD.

May the LORD bless you from Zion;
he who made heaven and earth.

{Standing and bowing}
Glory be to the Father, and to the Son, and to the Holy Spirit:

{Still standing but upright}
as it was in the beginning, is now, and ever shall be,
world without end. Amen.

All that said, pray in a position that feels reverent and allows you to focus on your interaction with your Lord and Savior.

WHAT IS ALL THIS BOWING STUFF ABOUT

The idea of bowing or kneeling as a posture of prayer or worship is at least as old as Abraham and, along with standing with arms extended, has been a part of Christian prayer and worship from the beginning.

In most of the traditions that have developed in the past couple hundred years, though, there isn't much bowing done any more other than an occasional directive to "bow your heads" at a prayer. This, of course, is a bow. In the Church, we call it a Simple Bow.

There is also what we call a Solemn Bow holding the hands together and bowing much more deeply from the waist. And of course, there is simply kneeling – on both knees or just one.

All of these positions are bodily actions of reverence.

When we teach bowing to children at the Mission, we start by asking them, "who is the King of all creation?" They of course, say, "Jesus." We then ask them, "and what do you do when you come before a king?" Usually, the first or second answer to this question is, "you bow." Exactly.

Of course, since the ascended Christ is everywhere present, we could bow in any direction as we bow to Christ. But at least for the sake of safety (heads banging together) and uniformity, in the Church we generally choose to bow toward a cross as the symbol of Christ's kingship.

You may not ever do a Solemn Bow while praying at home but it is worth taking a moment to ponder it, maybe explain the above to your children, so that any bow, simple, solemn, or kneeling, will be done with a proper reverence to the King.

ANOTHER WORD ABOUT PHYSICAL ACTIONS

For some of you, this discussion about physical actions may be uncomfortable or kind of new. It was for me when I first began learning about historical forms of Christian prayer and worship. So, I'd like to give you a few things to think about.

I'm an American, and I assume most of my readers probably will be as well. In the past few years there has been no shortage of discussion regarding kneeling during our national anthem. Regardless of our opinions about the actions of the athletes who were kneeling, we have all learned that the actions of our bodies during corporate ceremony is certainly NOT unimportant.

Standing (or kneeling), removing a hat, putting a hand over the heart, saluting, standing at attention, bowing, all these things demonstrate our convictions. You could say they "embody" our commitments.

At the school our Mission runs, we have Morning Prayer (with bowing) and we say the Pledge of Allegiance as well. We allow our staff to have any of three positions of conscience: 1) they can bow at prayer AND put their hand over their heart at the pledge; 2) they can neither bow NOR put their hand over their heart; or 3) they can only bow and NOT put their hand over their heart.

The one option we do not allow them is to not bow to Christ but to place their hand on their heart for the pledge. Either you believe in the embodiment of commitments or you do not. If they do, then their first and primary commitment will be to the Lord.

You may still not like the idea of bowing or kneeling, but I hope you'll consider these ideas a bit at least. Especially since we are about to start talking about "crossing yourself" and I don't want to lose you.

MAKING THE SIGN OF THE CROSS

This is one of the most ancient physical actions of Christian prayer. Apparently back in the early church, Christians used to make the sign of the cross over themselves all the time and over everything that they were about to eat, drink, wear, or do.

In the 200's A.D. a well known Christian thinker and writer wrote, ""In all our travels and movements, in all our coming in and going out, in putting on our shoes, at the bath, at the table, in lighting our candles, in lying down, in sitting down, whatever employment occupies us, we mark our foreheads with the sign of the cross."

Making the sign of the cross can be done by simply tracing a little cross on your forehead with your thumb or you can sign a larger cross over your body. To do this second way, start by holding your right thumb, index finger, and middle finger together. Then touch your forehead, then down to your navel, then touch your right shoulder, then the left.

If you're new to "crossing yourself" and are worried about doing it "backwards," the good news is - you can't. If you touch the left shoulder first and then the right, then you'll be in good company with half the Church. The Eastern Church goes right to left (pushers) and the Roman Church goes left to right (pullers). Some Anglicans do it one way, some the other. Once again, it's not magic.

Give it a try when no one's watching. When I first started, I probably did it a thousand times alone before I ever tried crossing myself in public worship. Totally unnecessary of course.

When you feel comfortable have the kids try. We often remind our daughter to "make your cross."

Additionally, when she was younger, we taught her that it is a simple prayer she can say anytime she wants to. The prayer goes "Father (touch the forehead), Son (navel), Holy Spirit (shoulders)." We told her that the prayer is to remind her that God is always with her and she can always call upon Him.

If you do decide to pray in this sort of way, the usual places when people would make the sign of the cross have been marked with a "†". However, you are neither limited to nor required to cross yourself at these times.

SAYING AMEN

The word "Amen" means in its original language pretty much what it means in English today. It is a statement of affirmation and agreement.

In the prayer life of the Church as a whole, as well as in individual families, it is always appropriate for everyone to say "Amen" whenever it is to be said. In saying "Amen," you are affirming that "what this person has just prayed is my prayer too."

WHAT ABOUT SINGING

Absolutely. Traditionally, the whole of these services would be sung, or chanted. Feel free to do so yourself. If you want to sing a hymn or some other spiritual song, the best place to do so would be just before or just after the lessons are read or in place of the Canticle (or sing the Canticle, the word means "song").

A VERY BRIEF HISTORY FOR THOSE WHO ARE INTERESTED

This history of the Daily Office goes back to Jewish prayer times. The first Christians were Jews and we read about them keeping the times of Jewish prayer in the Acts of the Apostles.

> *Acts 3:1 Now Peter and John were going up to the temple at the hour of prayer, the ninth hour. ESV*

> *Acts 10:9 The next day, as they were on their journey and approaching the city, Peter went up on the housetop about the sixth hour to pray. ESV*

> *Acts 10:30 And Cornelius said, "Four days ago, about this hour, I was praying in my house at the ninth hour, and behold, a man stood before me in bright clothing… ESV*

An important instruction for churches that was written before even some of the New Testament writings were written (it's called the *Didache*) mentions praying the Lord's Prayer three times a day.

And Church Fathers writing in the 100's and 200's A.D. speak of Morning and Evening Prayers and prayers at the traditional hours – the Third, Sixth, and Ninth hours of the day (9am, 12 noon, and 3pm for us more or less).

Over time, these prayer times developed and, especially in monastic settings, they developed quite extensively and complexly. They had eight formal times of prayer. This was based on Psalm 119: 62 & 164:

Psalm 119:62 At midnight I rise to praise you, because of your righteous rules. ESV

Psalm 119:164 Seven times a day I praise you for your righteous rules. ESV

In the 1500's, the Archbishop of Canturbury, Thomas Cranmer, compiled and simplified the monastic offices with the hope that they could once again become the prayers of the regular work-a-day Christian. He offered two prayer times: Morning Prayer and Evening Prayer.

Over the 500 years since then, most Anglican communities have added back in Mid-Day Prayer and Compline.

Historically, the Offices were primarily recitations of the Psalms with an Office of Readings in the Morning. Cranmer had the desire that everyone could hear all of the Scripture – and there was no mass production of affordable Bibles at the time – so he established a daily lectionary that went through the majority of Scripture in one year but required an Old and New Testament reading at both morning and evening. This would be done in the local parish so everyone had the chance to hear the whole of Scripture each year.

If you want to know more about the history of the Daily Offices, just search for it on the internet. There is a ton of information available.

SOME GUIDANCE ON FAMILY PRAYER

Often, a family prayer/devotional time is approached with the goals and values of a classroom or school. That is to say, we seek to offer verbal instruction that will engage the minds of our children with some new information about God, Christ, the Kingdom, etc.

There is a different way, one that is much older. This other way does not neglect the verbal instruction, rather it approaches the activity itself with different goals and values – more like the training of an athlete. We consider a figure skater to be excellent precisely because she has practiced the quadruple Axel every day for years. Her training is not in learning a new move every day but in practicing the same moves until performing them comes as naturally and easily as walking down the street.

This book is designed to assist your family in developing its "training routine." Instead of family prayer being something that we "say", or "prepare", or "listen to", we'd like for you to think of it primarily as an activity that you do together.

You'll find that each day is very much the same. You'll also find that your younger children want it to be even more the same every day than it is. There's a great deal of comfort for young kids in the familiarity of the repetition.

Even for us whose minds have been trained by the world around us to require new, stimulating information on a rapid basis, we will find the familiarity to be grounding, to be a strong tower, to be a place we can truly hide beneath the shadow of our Savior's wings. In the midst of chaotic daily routines, a habit of prayer can become an activity that cultivates stillness before God.

As you are seeking to develop a routine for your family, remember that there is not the "perfect" routine. Every family's rhythm is different.

Additionally, where in the life of your family that you are beginning this activity will determine in part how you get started. A family with all teenage children that has never had family prayer time will necessarily begin in a much different manner than a couple who is expecting their first child.

Begin how and when you can. Your family prayer will certainly develop as your family grows and changes. It will take a while for it to feel comfortable. It is a discipline after-all and disciplines can be hard. So, don't give up or change things too quickly.

Keeping all this in mind, below I have included some thoughts to help you think through some parts of your family prayer time. Involve the kids in the development. Have fun.

May God bless your efforts of creating a time for your family to gather together for the *activity* of prayer.

EVERYONE PARTICIPATES

I'd like to encourage you to find roles for everyone. As children are able to read, you can assign them particular parts that are theirs alone to offer to the time.

Give them their own prayer to say. When our daughter was three, we taught her this prayer that was hers:

"Thank you, Lord, for loving me and for loving the whole world. Amen."

Then we made a couple different places in the service when it is time for her to pray her prayer. Feel free to use this prayer yourself. Or make up another one.

Not everyone's participation has to be a solo reading or speaking part either. Perhaps you might light candles. The youngest child could set one out, the oldest child could light it, the middle child could blow it out afterwards. You can rotate these jobs.

The ritual of every household will be different but having some sort of ritual (however minor it may be) is important. I do not mean that it is important in the sense that having three rituals is somehow "holier" than one. I mean that it is important that every member of the family has something to offer to the family *activity* that you are doing together. Everyone contributes. This is a microcosm of the worship of the whole Church after all.

OTHER PERSONAL PRAYERS

After the response, "For only in you can we live in safety," some families may choose to let everyone have time to pray freely, whatever is on their heart.

Other families may not feel a need to do this as their hearts have been expressed through the rest of the service. Neither way is better than the other.

Whether or not this is done, there should be a brief silence kept before the concluding prayers. This is a time of simply sitting quietly in the presence of our Creator who loves us and who hears our prayers. Help your kids understand this.

YOUNG KIDS

There can be no standard rule of prayer that fits every family. As parents, you'll have to set reasonable expectations for your children in accordance with their age.

In our family, when our daughter was three, the rule was that she had to be still (not running around or climbing up and down on people), be quiet (not interrupting), and stay in the same room with us. She was allowed to look at one of her own books, or to color, or to play quietly with a toy. We encouraged her to do one of these things while sitting in one of our laps and she usually took the offer. Regardless of what else she may have been doing, she almost always participated in the repetitive parts.

Now that she is nine, we have a little more expectation of what it means for her to be respectful and to participate with what the family is doing together. But then, she has been doing this since she was in diapers. This won't be the same for the first day with your kid, no matter how old they are. Do what's right for your family.

In determining what you ask of your young children, it may be helpful to have these three guidelines: that they are valuably included, that the time is an enjoyable part of family life, and that the time is important to mom and dad.

PRAYING AS PARENTS

I'd like to expand upon this last point - that prayer is important to mom and dad. As every parent knows, our kids see through our charade. For this reason, our prayer time should be serious. This does not mean our prayer time should be not-fun. It means that our prayer time should be not-pretend.

Prayer can come across to our children as being "pretend" in many ways. One of the most unintentional or accidental ways that this can happen for parents is in the way that we speak to God. It is one thing to pray with a child's cadence and tone while helping your child to pray his or her own prayers. But we must be careful not to pray *our* own prayers in the same fashion. When we pray as adults, we should speak as adults speak.

Additionally, in planning a family prayer time, it may be necessary for each of us to spend some honest (and perhaps difficult) time examining ourselves, our lives, our marriage, our role as husband or wife, our priorities, and even our motivations for having family prayer.

None of these things should prevent us from starting a family prayer time. But perhaps starting a family prayer time may force us to realign certain parts of our lives with the claims that we make as followers of Jesus.

UNDERSTANDING THE FORM OF THE SERVICE

OPENING SENTENCES

In the Anglican tradition, Morning and Evening Prayer generally start with an opening sentence of Scripture and then Confession (discussed next). If you have a Book of Common Prayer (BCP), you can find some suggestions for opening Scripture in it if you like.

For a family service, this is a good place to have a child read a verse or to have everyone say together a verse you are working to memorize.

In this book, we are trying to simplify things to help you get started. For that reason, we start the service with the Opening Dialogue (see below).

CONFESSION

In the Anglican part of the Church it is the custom to say a confession at the beginning of Morning Prayer, Evening Prayer or both. Confession is the second step of repentance (the first step being the Lord's love and mercy). If we are to lead lives of repentance, then confession is a necessary part.

There are many different prayers of confession. We have included some at the beginning of this book (p. 32-37). You may use any of them as part of your regular habit of prayer. To do this, you would simply begin with the confession prayer, then the words of assurance, and then move into the regular service.

Compline generally starts with a confession across all traditions and so we have included a confession as part of the regular service there.

We have also included a litany for Christ's deliverance (p. 31) that is used by our mission. You may find it also to be a helpful prayer. We sing it at the beginning of our Sunday Eucharist liturgy every week.

OPENING DIALOGUE

All of the offices begin with the echo of Psalm 40:13 and Psalm 70:1, "O God, make speed to save [us], O Lord, make haste to help [us]."

Because in the past all of Psalm 51 would have been prayed in the early morning office (like, at midnight), Morning Prayer typically begins with Psalm 51:15, "Lord, open [our] lips, and [our] mouth shall proclaim your praise." Although in a family setting you probably have already said a few things in the day, in your private morning prayers this psalm is certainly a great first word of the day. What would happen if we said this before every opening of our mouth throughout the day?

The actual Psalms are in the singular though - "me, my" rather than "us, our". In your private prayers, you should feel free to say "me" and "my" – as in "O God, make speed to save *me*. O Lord, make haste to help *me*."

This opening dialogue, including the "Glory be," the reading of Scripture, and the Lord's Prayer are essentially what makes up the backbone of all the offices and of what we are calling "recollections" (p. 198-204) as well.

VENITE

This word is simply Latin for the first part of the Psalm, "O Come." All the Psalms and Canticles are named by the first word or two in Latin from back in the old days. The Venite is a traditional opening Psalm of Morning Prayer - at least back to the time of St. Benendict (500 AD).

There are a few different traditions on how the Venite goes. Some pray all of Psalm 95. Some leave off a part of the ending of Psalm 95. And some have an ending from Psalm 96. The way we do it here is a composite of these traditions.

READING THE PSALMS

Historically, the bulk of the Offices is praying the Psalms back to God.

It is great if, in a family prayer time, everyone can participate in the reading of the Psalm. Ideally, it would be read slowly and there would be a brief pause after each line.

Some families may choose to alternate verses. If a family chooses to alternate verses, everyone should say together the final "Glory be to the Father…"

Other families may want to have just one person read. That's fine too.

You might use the Psalm section to work on memorizing a Psalm together as a family and therefore you may choose to say the same Psalm every day for a while rather than saying a different one each day. A good psalm to start with is Saturday's Psalm, Psalm 23.

For private prayers, I recommend either choosing two or three Psalms that you are working to memorize or reading the Psalm offered in this book for each day and one or two other Psalms from either our lectionary or from some other way of going through all the Psalms regularly.

LESSONS

The services in this book can be used with any reading plan or daily "lectionary" (this word just means an order of reading through the Bible).

For Families with Young Children
We recommend *Sacred Stories of the Old and New Testament: Selected for Children*. This is a compilation of most of the narrative portions of the Bible or at least those that are not inappropriate for children.

It is the ESV Scripture, not a paraphrase or re-telling. Each story is presented as a one-or-two page chapter of the book with a title, a beginning, and an ending. It reads very much like a children's chapter book.

It is available at the**trinity**mission.org

For Going Through the Whole of Scripture
In your private prayers, it is suggested to have some plan of reading through all of Scripture regularly. This can be done with the "two bookmark method" – which is one bookmark in the Old Testament and one in the New Testament and just read a chapter or so from each each day.

If you would like a more intentional plan then we recommend The Trinity Mission's Daily Office lectionary resource, *Daily Readings for the Christian Year*. It too can be found at the**trinity**mission.org.

Daily Readings for the Christian Year will take you through *most** of the Bible in either one or two years (*some of the boundary descriptions and Old Testament genealogies are not included).

By using *Daily Readings for the Christian Year*, you will read through books of the Bible in a continuous fashion and yet have readings that are appropriate to the liturgical time of year being celebrated by the Church.

Additionally, the readings during the week help to illuminate the Sunday readings if your church uses the Revised Common Lectionary, the 1979 Book of Common Prayer Lectionary, the Roman Catholic Lectionary for Mass, or the ACNA Book of Common Prayer 2019 Sunday Lectionary.

Other Ideas
Different traditions have different reading plans, lectionaries, breviaries, etc. You can search online or talk with your pastor to find something that works for you.

CANTICLES

As I mentioned above, this word simply means "a song." Within the Benedictine and the Anglican prayerbook tradition there were certain canticles that were chanted at particular times of the day. Most of them were selections of Scripture that were written as songs within Scripture.

In this book, for Morning Prayer we rotate between two canticles. We start with the *Benedictus* (Latin for *Blessed*, the first word of the canticle) also known as the song Zechariah sung when his son John the Baptist was born. This canticle has the longer history of being part of Morning Prayer.

The other canticle we use is from the Revelation and is called *A Song to the Lamb*. It is shorter – which may make it easier for quick memorization. It also beautifully and succinctly encompasses all of the work that God is doing through Christ.

It is totally appropriate to only use one canticle for a season until you have it commited to memory.

CREED

There are two creeds generally used in the Western Church: that called the Apostles' Creed and that called the Nicene Creed. The shorter Apostles' Creed has a wider use in the Benedictine and Anglican Daily Office but the Nicene Creed is considered the sufficient statement of the Christian faith and is the creed that we hold in common with all Christians throughout the world, west and east.

It is also the creed that we say during the Eucharist. We have found that is unnecesarily difficult for people to try to memorize two different creeds with so many similar statements, one in the Offices and a different one at the Eucharist.

So, for both the reason of ease in memorization and a connection to the whole Church, we use the Nicene creed in our services.

KYRIE, LORD, HAVE MERCY

Lord, have mercy (*Kyrie eleison* in Greek, pronounced KEER-ree-ay e-LAY-ih-sohn) is an ancient Christian prayer and a complete prayer in and of itself. Often in our contemporary prayers we might use a phrase like "be with" as in "Lord, please *be with* mom during her surgery."

Of course, we all know that the Lord is present everywhere and that He loves all He has made and so He will naturally "be with" mom during her surgery. Asking Him to "be with" her is simply our way of expressing more than we can understand in desiring all of His sovereign Goodness to be present in that particular circumstance.

This older phrase, "Lord, have mercy," conveys all of this and perhaps even a bit more. It's asking for God's presence, for His action, for His goodness and mercy and love for His creation to be effected in that circumstance. It's a cry of helplessness, a confession that we do not know what to do, as well as a cry of trust - trust that God does know and can and will do it.

THE LORD'S PRAYER

The structure of the Offices that we present in this book is essentially the reading of Scripture and saying the Lord's Prayer. We use the traditional form of the Lord's Prayer because sadly, the authorized modern form lacks connection to our English-speaking heritage. If you don't like "Thees and Thous" and don't like the odd phrasing of the modern version in the prayer book, another possible way of modernizing the language of the traditional form might be:

> Our Father in heaven,
> hallowed be your Name,
> your kingdom come,
> your will be done,
> on earth as it is in heaven.
> Give us this day our daily bread.
> And forgive us our trespasses,

as we forgive those
who trespass against us.
And lead us not into temptation,
but deliver us from the evil one.
For yours is the kingdom,
and the power, and the glory,
for ever and ever. Amen.

INTERCESSIONS

The intercessions are the formal prayers we offer for all manner of things.
The intercessions we use in this book are broader and more particular than
those of the prayerbook and are better suited for private prayer as
individuals or families.

Following the formal prayers, you should offer your own free form
prayers to the Lord. In small groups, time should be given for everyone to
do the same even if it is done in silence.

SILENCE

Following the intercession prayers, a brief silence should be kept.
Obviously, in families with young children, this may be a very brief
silence. But even if brief, the silence will be good training for the children
that prayer is not always about us speaking.

COLLECTS

The Collects (pronounce with emphasis on the first syllable, COL-lect) is
a prayer that one person says on behalf of everyone, a *collective* prayer
you might say. They follow a particular form that is worth learning if you
decide to try your hand at writing Collects for your family.

These prayers are usually said by the Leader and everyone, as always, should say the "Amen." Your family may choose to say the Collects all together or to have a different person say a collect each day of the week.

You will see an instruction that says, "The Collect of the Week may be said." This is referring to the Collect that was said for the preceeding Sunday at Church. If you don't know what that is, then you can just skip it for now. We have a separate resource that comes out yearly with the readings and collects for every day of the year. Check on the website if you are interested in that.

GENERAL THANKSGIVING

If you choose to say the General Thanksgiving, this is usually said by everyone together. It is a great prayer to memorize and have on hand for throughout your day.

FINAL BLESSING

There are many ways to conclude and ask God's blessing on yourself and your family. The one we offer here is the typical Bendictine/Anglican blessing... "May the Grace of our Lord Jesus Christ..."

Sometimes in my own morning prayers, I will follow the traditional blessing with the following (making a small cross on my mouth, my forehead, and my heart):

May the words of my †mouth and the †meditation of my †heart be pleasing in your sight, O Lord, my rock and my redeemer.

In the Name of the †Father, and of the Son, and of the Holy Spirit, I go into this day.

Glory to you Lord Jesus Christ. Glory forever.

How to Use the Rest of this Book

The rest of this book consists of the actual texts for the services. There is a separate text for Morning Prayer for each day of the week, then for Mid-day Prayer for each day of the week, and also for Evening prayer for each day of the week. There is only one text for the service of Compline but there is a set of readings for each day of the week in it.

You may want to start by just doing one Office a day. As you use these texts, you will get a sense for what things change each day and what things stay the same.

I encourage you to work toward committing to heart the parts that stay the same. When I teach about liturgy, I tell people that as long as you still need a book, you have not yet fully participated in what liturgy is supposed to be.

Toward the end of this book you will find what we have called "brief recollections." These are just the basic, stripped-down structure of the service with a bunch of directions *in italics* explaining how you might add in more parts depending on how much time you have. Once you are familiar with the services in their fuller form, you will have a pretty good sense of what you might want to add back in.

These brief recollections are good for having some sort of short prayer time throughout the day even if you may not have time in your schedule for the full Office.

And then finally, at the end of the book you will find two texts. One is called "A General Structure for Family Prayer" and the other is called "A Form for Private Prayer."

The "General Structure for Family Prayer" is intended to give you a guideline or format to follow for putting together a family prayer time in accordance with the historic Daily Office form. Like the brief recollections, the basic structure is printed out in full and the rest of the text is directions as to what you might want to include also. This allows your family to pray in accordance with the Daily Office but to tailor it to the ages of your family and your particular life situation.

The final text, "A Form for Private Prayer," is the full Morning Prayer office as it could be used by an individual in their private prayers. This is the structure more or less that I follow myself and encourage others to do the same.

As has been said already, this book and the services and other resources available online at the**trinity**mission.org are tools for helping you and your household to develop a meaningful and fruitful habit of daily prayer.

The forms of prayer in here will be like a human skeleton; the structure will be basically the same but in each household the flesh will look a little different. Learn from what is here – make it your own.

I highly recommend that you set some reminder to come back and re-read these "Getting Started" pages again after you have been going for a few weeks. I think you will find the second and third time reading through will be of great help.

It is my prayer that everything here will help you to form yourself and your family into the likeness of Christ, to move you all deeper into intimacy with the God of all Creation, Father, Son, and Holy Spirit.

Glory to Jesus Christ,
-mtj

A
LITANY
AND
VARIOUS
CONFESSIONS

A Short Litany for Christ's Deliverance

Lord, have mercy.
Christ, have mercy.
Lord, have mercy.

From all selfish desires;
from pride, vanity, and hypocrisy;
from envy, hatred, and malice;
and from all evil intent; in your mercy...
Lord Jesus Christ, deliver us.

From laziness, worldliness, and love of money;
from hardness of heart
and contempt for your Word and your laws,
from seeking our own aims and glory
rather than your Kingdom;
in your mercy...
Lord Jesus Christ, deliver us.

From sins of body and mind;
from deceits of the world, the flesh, and the devil;
in your mercy...
Lord Jesus Christ, deliver us.

Lord, have mercy.
Christ, have mercy.
Lord, have mercy.

Confession from Prayerbook - 1662

ALMIGHTY and most merciful Father,
We have erred, and strayed from thy ways like lost sheep,
We have followed too much the devices and desires of our own hearts,
We have offended against thy holy laws,
We have left undone those things which we ought to have done,
And we have done those things which we ought not to have done,
And there is no health in us:
But thou, O Lord, have mercy upon us miserable offenders;
Spare thou them, O God, which confess their faults,
Restore thou them who are penitent,
According to thy promises declared unto mankind
in Christ Jesu our Lord:
And grant, O most merciful Father, for his sake,
That we may hereafter live a godly, righteous, and sober life,
To the glory of thy holy Name.
Amen.

Confession from Prayerbook - 1928 (US)

ALMIGHTY and most merciful Father;
We have erred, and strayed from thy ways like lost sheep.
We have followed too much the devices and desires of our own hearts.
We have offended against thy holy laws.
We have left undone those things which we ought to have done;
And we have done those things which we ought not to have done;
And there is no health in us.
But thou, O Lord, have mercy upon us, miserable offenders.
Spare thou those, O God, who confess their faults.
Restore thou those who are penitent;
According to thy promises declared unto mankind
In Christ Jesus our Lord.
And grant, O most merciful Father, for his sake;
That we may hereafter live a godly, righteous, and sober life,
To the glory of thy holy Name.
Amen.

Confession from Prayerbook - 1962 (Canada)

ALMIGHTY and most merciful Father,
We have erred, and strayed from thy ways like lost sheep,
We have followed too much the devices and desires of our own hearts,
We have offended against thy holy laws,
We have left undone those things which we ought to have done,
And we have done those things which we ought not to have done;
And there is no health in us.
But thou, O Lord, have mercy upon us, miserable offenders.
Spare thou them, O God, which confess their faults.
Restore thou them who are penitent;
According to thy promises declared unto mankind
in Christ Jesu our Lord.
And grant, O most merciful Father, for his sake,
That we may hereafter live a godly, righteous, and sober life,
To the glory of thy holy Name.
Amen.

Confession from Prayerbook - 1979 (US) Rite I

Almighty and most merciful Father,
we have erred and strayed from thy ways like lost sheep,
we have followed too much the devices and desires of our own hearts,
we have offended against thy holy laws,
we have left undone those things which we ought to have done,
and we have done those things which we ought not to have done.
But thou, O Lord, have mercy upon us,
spare thou those who confess their faults,
restore thou those who are penitent,
according to thy promises declared unto mankind
in Christ Jesus our Lord;
and grant, O most merciful Father, for his sake,
that we may hereafter live a godly, righteous, and sober life,
to the glory of thy holy Name. Amen

A brief silence is kept

The Almighty and merciful Lord grant us absolution and remission of all
our sins, true repentance, amendment of life, and the grace and
consolation of his Holy Spirit. Amen.

Confession from Prayerbook - 1979 (US) Rite II

Most merciful God,
we confess that we have sinned against you
in thought, word, and deed,
by what we have done,
and by what we have left undone.
We have not loved you with our whole heart;
we have not loved our neighbors as ourselves.
We are truly sorry and we humbly repent.
For the sake of your Son Jesus Christ,
have mercy on us and forgive us;
that we may delight in your will,
and walk in your ways,
to the glory of your Name. Amen.

A brief silence is kept

Almighty God have mercy on us, forgive us all our sins through our Lord
Jesus Christ, strengthen us in all goodness, and by the power of the Holy
Spirit keep us in eternal life. Amen.

Confession from Prayerbook – 2019 (US)

Almighty and most merciful Father,
we have erred and strayed from your ways like lost sheep.
We have followed too much the devices and desires
    of our own hearts.
We have offended against your holy laws.
We have left undone those things which we ought to have
    done,
and we have done those things which we ought not
    to have done;
and apart from your grace, there is no health in us.
O Lord, have mercy upon us.
Spare all those who confess their faults.
Restore all those who are penitent,
    according to your promises declared to all people in
    Christ Jesus our Lord.
And grant, O most merciful Father, for his sake,
that we may now live a godly, righteous, and sober life,
to the glory of your holy Name. Amen.

A brief silence is kept

Grant your faithful people, merciful Lord, pardon and peace; that we may
be cleansed from all our sins, and serve you with a quiet mind; through
Jesus Christ our Lord. Amen.

MORNING PRAYER

Sunday
Morning Prayer

Officiant	† Lord, open our lips.
All	**And our mouth shall proclaim your praise.**
Officiant	† O God, make speed to save us.
All	**O Lord, make haste to help us.**

† Glory be to the Father, and to the Son, and to the Holy Spirit; as it was in the beginning, is now, and ever shall be; world without end. Amen.

Venite *O Come*
Psalm 95:1-8; 96:9,13

O come, let us sing to the Lord;
let us shout for joy to the Rock of our salvation.
Let us come before his presence with thanksgiving
and raise a loud shout to him with psalms.

For the Lord is a great God,
and a great King above all gods.
In his hand are the caverns of the earth,
and the heights of the hills are his also.

The sea is his, for he made it,
and his hands have molded the dry land.
O come, let us worship and bow down,
and kneel before the Lord our Maker.

For he is our God,
and we are the people of his pasture and the sheep of his hand.
Today, if you hear his voice,
Do not harden your heart, as in the rebellion.

O worship the Lord in the beauty of holiness;
let the whole earth stand in awe of him.
For he comes, for he comes to judge the earth
and with righteousness to judge the world
and the peoples in his faithfulness.

A Psalm Appointed for Sundays
The following or some other psalm may be said.

Psalm 126

When the LORD restored the fortunes of Zion,
we were like those who dream.

Our mouths were filled with laughter then,
and our tongues with shouts of joy;

Then they said among the nations,
"The LORD has done great things for them."

The LORD has done great things for us;
and we are glad indeed.

Restore our fortunes, O LORD,
like streams in the Negev!

Those who sow in tears
shall reap with shouts of joy!

He who goes out weeping,
carrying the seed to sow,

Will surely come again with shouts of joy,
carrying his sheaves with him.

At the end of the Psalms is said
† Glory be to the Father, and to the Son, and to the Holy Spirit:
as it was in the beginning, is now, and ever shall be,
world without end. Amen.

The Lessons
*One or two Lessons from Scripture may be read. The following Canticle
may be sung or said between or after the Lessons.*

The Song of Zechariah
Benedictus Dominus Deus
Luke 1: 68-79

Blessed be the Lord, the God of Israel;
he has come to his people and set them free.

He has raised up for us a mighty savior,
born of the house of his servant David.

Through his holy prophets he promised of old,
that he would save us from our enemies,
from the hands of all who hate us.

He promised to show mercy to our fathers
and to remember his holy covenant.

This was the oath he swore to our father Abraham,
to set us free from the hands of our enemies,

Free to worship him without fear,
holy and righteous in his sight
all the days of our life.

You, my child, shall be called the prophet of the Most High,
for you will go before the Lord to prepare his way,

To give his people knowledge of salvation
by the forgiveness of their sins.

In the tender compassion of our God
the dawn from on high shall break upon us,

To shine on those who dwell in darkness
and the shadow of death,
and to guide our feet into the way of peace.

† Glory be to the Father, and to the Son, and to the Holy Spirit:
as it was in the beginning, is now, and ever shall be,
world without end. Amen.

The Creed

I believe in one God,
    the Father, the Almighty,
    maker of heaven and earth,
    of all that is, visible and invisible.

I believe in one Lord, Jesus Christ,
    the only-begotten Son of God,
    eternally begotten of the Father,
    God from God, Light from Light,
    true God from true God,
    begotten, not made,
    of one Being with the Father;
    through him all things were made.
For us and for our salvation he came down from heaven,
    was incarnate from the Holy Spirit and the Virgin Mary,
    and was made man.
For our sake he was crucified under Pontius Pilate;
    he suffered death and was buried.
On the third day he rose again in accordance with the Scriptures;
    he ascended into heaven
    and is seated at the right hand of the Father.
He will come again in glory to judge the living and the dead,
    and his kingdom will have no end.

I believe in the Holy Spirit, the Lord, the giver of life,
    who proceeds from the Father,
    who with the Father and the Son is worshiped and glorified,
    who has spoken through the prophets.
I believe in one holy catholic and apostolic Church.
I acknowledge one Baptism for the forgiveness of sins.
I look for the resurrection of the dead,
    † and the life of the world to come. Amen.

Officiant	Lord have mercy (upon us).
All	**Christ have mercy.**
	Lord have mercy.

Our Father, who art in heaven,
hallowed be thy Name,
thy kingdom come,
thy will be done,
on earth as it is in heaven.
Give us this day our daily bread.
And forgive us our trespasses,
as we forgive those
who trespass against us.
And lead us not into temptation,
but deliver us from evil.
For thine is the kingdom,
and the power, and the glory,
for ever and ever. Amen.

Officiant	God of all creation, full of love and abounding in mercy;
All	**May the whole earth be filled with your glory.**
Officiant	Lord, bless and guide all ministers of your church;
All	**Clothe them in righteousness and grant them wisdom.**
Officiant	Direct the leaders of our nation;
All	**That they may act in accordance with your kingdom.**
Officiant	Enlarge our own hearts, O Lord,
All	**To love the things that you love.**
Officiant	May we proclaim your light
All	**In every place where there is darkness.**

Officiant	May we proclaim your Holy Name
All	**In every aspect of our lives.**
Officiant	Create in us clean hearts, O God;
All	**And renew a right spirit within us.**
Officiant	Grant us your peace;
All	**For only in you can we live in safety.**
Officiant	We pray for those in sickness, grief, persecution, bondage, fear, and loneliness;
All	**Lord, have mercy.**

(pause to offer your own prayers or to sit in silence)

Collects
The Collect for the week may be said. Then,

Collect for Strength

O God our King, by the resurrection of your Son Jesus Christ on the first day of the week, you conquered sin, put death to flight, and gave us the hope of everlasting life: Redeem all our days by this victory; forgive our sins, banish our fears, make us bold to praise you and to do your will; and steel us to wait for the consummation of your kingdom on the last great Day; through the same Jesus Christ our Lord. *Amen.*

Prayer for Sundays

O God, you make us glad with the weekly remembrance of the glorious resurrection of your Son our Lord: Give us this day such blessing through our worship of you, that the week to come may be spent in your favor; through Jesus Christ our Lord. *Amen.*

General Thanksgiving (said together)

Almighty God, Father of all mercies,
we your unworthy servants give you humble thanks
for all your goodness and loving-kindness
to us and to all whom you have made.
We bless you for our creation, preservation,
and all the blessings of this life;
but above all for your immeasurable love
in the redemption of the world by our Lord Jesus Christ;
for the means of grace, and for the hope of glory.
And, we pray, give us such an awareness of your mercies,
that with truly thankful hearts
we may show forth your praise,
not only with our lips, but in our lives,
by giving up our selves to your service,
and by walking before you
in holiness and righteousness all our days;
through Jesus Christ our Lord,
to whom, with you and the Holy Spirit,
be honor and glory throughout all ages. Amen.

Officiant	Let us bless the Lord.
All	**Thanks be to God.**

Officiant   † The grace of our Lord Jesus Christ, and the love of
God, and the fellowship of the Holy Spirit, be with us all
evermore. Amen.
2 Corinthians 13:14

Monday
Morning Prayer

Officiant	† Lord, open our lips.
All	**And our mouth shall proclaim your praise.**
Officiant	† O God, make speed to save us.
All	**O Lord, make haste to help us.**

† Glory be to the Father, and to the Son, and to the Holy Spirit; as it was in the beginning, is now, and ever shall be; world without end. Amen.

Venite *O Come*
Psalm 95:1-8; 96:9,13

O come, let us sing to the Lord;
let us shout for joy to the Rock of our salvation.
Let us come before his presence with thanksgiving
and raise a loud shout to him with psalms.

For the Lord is a great God,
and a great King above all gods.
In his hand are the caverns of the earth,
and the heights of the hills are his also.

The sea is his, for he made it,
and his hands have molded the dry land.
O come, let us worship and bow down,
and kneel before the Lord our Maker.

For he is our God,
and we are the people of his pasture and the sheep of his hand.
Today, if you hear his voice,
Do not harden your heart, as in the rebellion.

O worship the Lord in the beauty of holiness;
let the whole earth stand in awe of him.
For he comes, for he comes to judge the earth
and with righteousness to judge the world
and the peoples in his faithfulness.

A Psalm Appointed for Mondays
The following or some other psalm may be said.

Psalm 8

O LORD, our Lord,
how majestic is your Name in all the earth!
You have set your glory above the heavens.

Out of the mouth of infants and babes you have ordained praise,
because of your adversaries, to silence the enemy and the avenger.

When I consider your heavens, the work of your fingers,
the moon and the stars, which you have ordained,

What is man that you are mindful of him,
the son of man that you care for him?

Yet you have made him a little lower than the angels
and crowned him with glory and honor.

You have given him dominion over the works of your hands;
you have put all things under his feet,

All sheep and oxen,
and the beasts of the field,

The birds of the heavens, and the fish of the sea,
all that passes along the paths of the seas.

O LORD, our Lord,
how majestic is your Name in all the earth!

At the end of the Psalms is said
† Glory be to the Father, and to the Son, and to the Holy Spirit:
as it was in the beginning, is now, and ever shall be,
world without end. Amen.

The Lessons
One or two Lessons from Scripture may be read. The following Canticle may be sung or said between or after the Lessons.

A Song to the Lamb
Dignus es
Revelation 4:11; 5:9-10, 13

Splendor and honor and kingly power
are yours by right, O Lord our God,

For you created everything that is,
and by your will they were created and have their being;

And yours by right, O Lamb that was slain,
for with your blood you have redeemed for God,

From every family, language, people, and nation,
a kingdom of priests to serve our God.

And so, to him who sits upon the throne,
and to Christ the Lamb,

Be worship and praise, dominion and splendor,
for ever and for evermore.

The Creed

I believe in one God,
> the Father, the Almighty,
> maker of heaven and earth,
> of all that is, visible and invisible.

I believe in one Lord, Jesus Christ,
> the only-begotten Son of God,
> eternally begotten of the Father,
> God from God, Light from Light,
> true God from true God,
> begotten, not made,
> of one Being with the Father;
> through him all things were made.

For us and for our salvation he came down from heaven,
> was incarnate from the Holy Spirit and the Virgin Mary,
> and was made man.

For our sake he was crucified under Pontius Pilate;
> he suffered death and was buried.

On the third day he rose again in accordance with the Scriptures;
> he ascended into heaven
> and is seated at the right hand of the Father.

He will come again in glory to judge the living and the dead,
> and his kingdom will have no end.

I believe in the Holy Spirit, the Lord, the giver of life,
> who proceeds from the Father,
> who with the Father and the Son is worshiped and glorified,
> who has spoken through the prophets.

I believe in one holy catholic and apostolic Church.

I acknowledge one Baptism for the forgiveness of sins.

I look for the resurrection of the dead,
> † and the life of the world to come. Amen.

Officiant	Lord have mercy (upon us).
All	**Christ have mercy.**
	Lord have mercy.

Our Father, who art in heaven,
hallowed be thy Name,
thy kingdom come,
thy will be done,
on earth as it is in heaven.
Give us this day our daily bread.
And forgive us our trespasses,
as we forgive those
who trespass against us.
And lead us not into temptation,
but deliver us from evil.
For thine is the kingdom,
and the power, and the glory,
for ever and ever. Amen.

Officiant	God of all creation, full of love and abounding in mercy;
All	**May the whole earth be filled with your glory.**
Officiant	Lord, bless and guide all ministers of your church;
All	**Clothe them in righteousness and grant them wisdom.**
Officiant	Direct the leaders of our nation;
All	**That they may act in accordance with your kingdom.**
Officiant	Enlarge our own hearts, O Lord,
All	**To love the things that you love.**
Officiant	May we proclaim your light
All	**In every place where there is darkness.**

Officiant	May we proclaim your Holy Name
All	**In every aspect of our lives.**
Officiant	Create in us clean hearts, O God;
All	**And renew a right spirit within us.**
Officiant	Grant us your peace;
All	**For only in you can we live in safety.**
Officiant	We pray for those in sickness, grief, persecution, bondage, fear, and loneliness;
All	**Lord, have mercy.**

(pause to offer your own prayers or to sit in silence)

Collects
The Collect for the week may be said. Then,

Collect for Renewal of Life

O God, the King eternal, whose light divides the day from the night and turns the shadow of death into the morning: Drive far from us all wrong desires, incline our hearts to keep your law, and guide our feet into the way of peace; that, having done your will with cheerfulness during the day, we may, when night comes, rejoice to give you thanks; through Jesus Christ our Lord. *Amen.*

Prayer for Mission

O God, you have made of one blood all the peoples of the earth, and sent your blessed Son to preach peace to those who are far off and to those who are near: Grant that people everywhere may seek after you and find you; bring the nations into your fold; pour out your Spirit upon all flesh; and hasten the coming of your kingdom; through Jesus Christ our Lord. *Amen.*

General Thanksgiving (said together)

Almighty God, Father of all mercies,
we your unworthy servants give you humble thanks
for all your goodness and loving-kindness
to us and to all whom you have made.
We bless you for our creation, preservation,
and all the blessings of this life;
but above all for your immeasurable love
in the redemption of the world by our Lord Jesus Christ;
for the means of grace, and for the hope of glory.
And, we pray, give us such an awareness of your mercies,
that with truly thankful hearts
we may show forth your praise,
not only with our lips, but in our lives,
by giving up our selves to your service,
and by walking before you
in holiness and righteousness all our days;
through Jesus Christ our Lord,
to whom, with you and the Holy Spirit,
be honor and glory throughout all ages. Amen.

Officiant	Let us bless the Lord.
All	**Thanks be to God.**
Officiant	† The grace of our Lord Jesus Christ, and the love of God, and the fellowship of the Holy Spirit, be with us all evermore. Amen. *2 Corinthians 13:14*

Tuesday
Morning Prayer

Officiant † Lord, open our lips.
All **And our mouth shall proclaim your praise.**

Officiant † O God, make speed to save us.
All **O Lord, make haste to help us.**

† Glory be to the Father, and to the Son, and to the Holy Spirit; as it was in the beginning, is now, and ever shall be; world without end. Amen.

Venite *O Come*
Psalm 95:1-8; 96:9,13

O come, let us sing to the Lord;
let us shout for joy to the Rock of our salvation.
Let us come before his presence with thanksgiving
and raise a loud shout to him with psalms.

For the Lord is a great God,
and a great King above all gods.
In his hand are the caverns of the earth,
and the heights of the hills are his also.

The sea is his, for he made it,
and his hands have molded the dry land.
O come, let us worship and bow down,
and kneel before the Lord our Maker.

For he is our God,
and we are the people of his pasture and the sheep of his hand.
Today, if you hear his voice,
Do not harden your heart, as in the rebellion.

O worship the Lord in the beauty of holiness;
let the whole earth stand in awe of him.
For he comes, for he comes to judge the earth
and with righteousness to judge the world
and the peoples in his faithfulness.

A Psalm Appointed for Tuesdays
The following or some other psalm may be said.

Psalm 32

Blessed are they whose transgressions are forgiven,
whose sin is covered.

Blessed is the man against whom the LORD counts no iniquity,
and in whose spirit there is no deceit.

When I kept silent, my bones wasted away
through my groaning all the day long.

For day and night your hand was heavy upon me;
my strength was dried up as in the heat of summer.

Then I acknowledged my sin to you,
and I did not cover up my iniquity;

I said, "I will confess my transgressions to the LORD,"
and you forgave me the guilt of my sin.

Therefore let everyone who is godly
offer prayer to you at the time when you may be found;

Surely in the rush of great waters,
they shall not reach him.

You are my hiding place;
you preserve me from trouble;
you surround me with songs of deliverance.

I will instruct you and teach you in the way you should go;
I will counsel you with my eye upon you.

Do not be like the horse or the mule, with no understanding,
which must be harnessed with bit and bridle,
or else it will not stay near you.

Many are the sorrows of the wicked,
but steadfast love surrounds the one who trusts in the LORD.

Be glad in the LORD, and rejoice, O you righteous,
sing, all you upright in heart!

At the end of the Psalms is said
† Glory be to the Father, and to the Son, and to the Holy Spirit:
as it was in the beginning, is now, and ever shall be,
world without end. Amen.

The Lessons
*One or two Lessons from Scripture may be read. The following Canticle
may be sung or said between or after the Lessons.*

The Song of Zechariah
Benedictus Dominus Deus
Luke 1: 68-79

Blessed be the Lord, the God of Israel;
he has come to his people and set them free.

He has raised up for us a mighty savior,
born of the house of his servant David.

Through his holy prophets he promised of old,
that he would save us from our enemies,
from the hands of all who hate us.

He promised to show mercy to our fathers
and to remember his holy covenant.

This was the oath he swore to our father Abraham,
to set us free from the hands of our enemies,

Free to worship him without fear,
holy and righteous in his sight
all the days of our life.

You, my child, shall be called the prophet of the Most High,
for you will go before the Lord to prepare his way,

To give his people knowledge of salvation
by the forgiveness of their sins.

In the tender compassion of our God
the dawn from on high shall break upon us,

To shine on those who dwell in darkness
and the shadow of death,
and to guide our feet into the way of peace.

† Glory be to the Father, and to the Son, and to the Holy Spirit:
as it was in the beginning, is now, and ever shall be,
world without end. Amen.

The Creed

I believe in one God,
    the Father, the Almighty,
    maker of heaven and earth,
    of all that is, visible and invisible.

I believe in one Lord, Jesus Christ,
    the only-begotten Son of God,
    eternally begotten of the Father,
    God from God, Light from Light,
    true God from true God,
    begotten, not made,
    of one Being with the Father;
    through him all things were made.
For us and for our salvation he came down from heaven,
    was incarnate from the Holy Spirit and the Virgin Mary,
    and was made man.
For our sake he was crucified under Pontius Pilate;
    he suffered death and was buried.
On the third day he rose again in accordance with the Scriptures;
    he ascended into heaven
    and is seated at the right hand of the Father.
He will come again in glory to judge the living and the dead,
    and his kingdom will have no end.

I believe in the Holy Spirit, the Lord, the giver of life,
    who proceeds from the Father,
    who with the Father and the Son is worshiped and glorified,
    who has spoken through the prophets.
I believe in one holy catholic and apostolic Church.
I acknowledge one Baptism for the forgiveness of sins.
I look for the resurrection of the dead,
    † and the life of the world to come. Amen.

Officiant	Lord have mercy (upon us).
All	**Christ have mercy.**
	Lord have mercy.

**Our Father, who art in heaven,
hallowed be thy Name,
thy kingdom come,
thy will be done,
on earth as it is in heaven.
Give us this day our daily bread.
And forgive us our trespasses,
as we forgive those
who trespass against us.
And lead us not into temptation,
but deliver us from evil.
For thine is the kingdom,
and the power, and the glory,
for ever and ever. Amen.**

Officiant	God of all creation, full of love and abounding in mercy;
All	**May the whole earth be filled with your glory.**
Officiant	Lord, bless and guide all ministers of your church;
All	**Clothe them in righteousness and grant them wisdom.**
Officiant	Direct the leaders of our nation;
All	**That they may act in accordance with your kingdom.**
Officiant	Enlarge our own hearts, O Lord,
All	**To love the things that you love.**
Officiant	May we proclaim your light
All	**In every place where there is darkness.**

Officiant	May we proclaim your Holy Name
All	**In every aspect of our lives.**
Officiant	Create in us clean hearts, O God;
All	**And renew a right spirit within us.**
Officiant	Grant us your peace;
All	**For only in you can we live in safety.**
Officiant	We pray for those in sickness, grief, persecution, bondage, fear, and loneliness;
All	**Lord, have mercy.**

(pause to offer your own prayers or to sit in silence)

Collects
The Collect for the week may be said. Then,

Collect for Peace

O God, the author of peace and lover of concord, to know you is eternal life and to serve you is perfect freedom: Defend us, your humble servants, in all assaults of our enemies; that we, surely trusting in your defense, may not fear the power of any adversaries; through the might of Jesus Christ our Lord. *Amen.*

Prayer for Mission

Almighty and everlasting God, by whose Spirit the whole body of your faithful people is governed and sanctified: Receive our supplications and prayers which we offer before you for all members of your holy Church, that in their vocation and ministry they may truly and devoutly serve you; through our Lord and Savior Jesus Christ. *Amen.*

General Thanksgiving (said together)

Almighty God, Father of all mercies,
we your unworthy servants give you humble thanks
for all your goodness and loving-kindness
to us and to all whom you have made.
We bless you for our creation, preservation,
and all the blessings of this life;
but above all for your immeasurable love
in the redemption of the world by our Lord Jesus Christ;
for the means of grace, and for the hope of glory.
And, we pray, give us such an awareness of your mercies,
that with truly thankful hearts
we may show forth your praise,
not only with our lips, but in our lives,
by giving up our selves to your service,
and by walking before you
in holiness and righteousness all our days;
through Jesus Christ our Lord,
to whom, with you and the Holy Spirit,
be honor and glory throughout all ages. Amen.

Officiant	Let us bless the Lord.
All	**Thanks be to God.**

Officiant   † The grace of our Lord Jesus Christ, and the love of
God, and the fellowship of the Holy Spirit, be with us all
evermore. Amen.
2 Corinthians 13:14

Wednesday
<u>Morning Prayer</u>

Officiant	† Lord, open our lips.
All	**And our mouth shall proclaim your praise.**

Officiant	† O God, make speed to save us.
All	**O Lord, make haste to help us.**

† Glory be to the Father, and to the Son, and to the Holy Spirit; as it was in the beginning, is now, and ever shall be; world without end. Amen.

Venite *O Come*
Psalm 95:1-8; 96:9,13

O come, let us sing to the Lord;
let us shout for joy to the Rock of our salvation.
Let us come before his presence with thanksgiving
and raise a loud shout to him with psalms.

For the Lord is a great God,
and a great King above all gods.
In his hand are the caverns of the earth,
and the heights of the hills are his also.

The sea is his, for he made it,
and his hands have molded the dry land.
O come, let us worship and bow down,
and kneel before the Lord our Maker.

For he is our God,
and we are the people of his pasture and the sheep of his hand.
Today, if you hear his voice,
Do not harden your heart, as in the rebellion.

O worship the Lord in the beauty of holiness;
let the whole earth stand in awe of him.
For he comes, for he comes to judge the earth
and with righteousness to judge the world
and the peoples in his faithfulness.

A Psalm Appointed for Wednesdays
The following or some other psalm may be said.

Psalm 63:1-7

O God, you are my God;
earnestly I seek you;

My soul thirsts for you;
my flesh faints for you,
in a dry and weary land
where there is no water.

So I have seen you in the sanctuary,
and beheld your power and your glory.

Because your love is better than life,
my lips will praise you.

So I will bless you as long as I live,
and in your Name I will lift up my hands.

My soul shall be satisfied as with the richest of foods,
and with joyful lips my mouth shall praise you,

When I remember you upon my bed,
and meditate on you through the watches of the night.

Because you have been my help,
I will sing for joy in the shadow of your wings.

At the end of the Psalms is said
† Glory be to the Father, and to the Son, and to the Holy Spirit:
as it was in the beginning, is now, and ever shall be,
world without end. Amen.

The Lessons

One or two Lessons from Scripture may be read. The following Canticle may be sung or said between or after the Lessons.

A Song to the Lamb
Dignus es
Revelation 4:11; 5:9-10, 13

Splendor and honor and kingly power
are yours by right, O Lord our God,

For you created everything that is,
and by your will they were created and have their being;

And yours by right, O Lamb that was slain,
for with your blood you have redeemed for God,

From every family, language, people, and nation,
a kingdom of priests to serve our God.

And so, to him who sits upon the throne,
and to Christ the Lamb,

Be worship and praise, dominion and splendor,
for ever and for evermore.

The Creed

I believe in one God,
    the Father, the Almighty,
    maker of heaven and earth,
    of all that is, visible and invisible.

I believe in one Lord, Jesus Christ,
    the only-begotten Son of God,
    eternally begotten of the Father,
    God from God, Light from Light,
    true God from true God,
    begotten, not made,
    of one Being with the Father;
    through him all things were made.
For us and for our salvation he came down from heaven,
    was incarnate from the Holy Spirit and the Virgin Mary,
    and was made man.
For our sake he was crucified under Pontius Pilate;
    he suffered death and was buried.
On the third day he rose again in accordance with the Scriptures;
    he ascended into heaven
    and is seated at the right hand of the Father.
He will come again in glory to judge the living and the dead,
    and his kingdom will have no end.

I believe in the Holy Spirit, the Lord, the giver of life,
    who proceeds from the Father,
    who with the Father and the Son is worshiped and glorified,
    who has spoken through the prophets.
I believe in one holy catholic and apostolic Church.
I acknowledge one Baptism for the forgiveness of sins.
I look for the resurrection of the dead,
    † and the life of the world to come. Amen.

Officiant	Lord have mercy (upon us).
All	**Christ have mercy.**
	Lord have mercy.

Our Father, who art in heaven,
hallowed be thy Name,
thy kingdom come,
thy will be done,
on earth as it is in heaven.
Give us this day our daily bread.
And forgive us our trespasses,
as we forgive those
who trespass against us.
And lead us not into temptation,
but deliver us from evil.
For thine is the kingdom,
and the power, and the glory,
for ever and ever. Amen.

Officiant	God of all creation, full of love and abounding in mercy;
All	**May the whole earth be filled with your glory.**
Officiant	Lord, bless and guide all ministers of your church;
All	**Clothe them in righteousness and grant them wisdom.**
Officiant	Direct the leaders of our nation;
All	**That they may act in accordance with your kingdom.**
Officiant	Enlarge our own hearts, O Lord,
All	**To love the things that you love.**
Officiant	May we proclaim your light
All	**In every place where there is darkness.**

Officiant	May we proclaim your Holy Name
All	**In every aspect of our lives.**
Officiant	Create in us clean hearts, O God;
All	**And renew a right spirit within us.**
Officiant	Grant us your peace;
All	**For only in you can we live in safety.**
Officiant	We pray for those in sickness, grief, persecution, bondage, fear, and loneliness;
All	**Lord, have mercy.**

(pause to offer your own prayers or to sit in silence)

Collects
The Collect for the week may be said. Then,

Collect for Grace

Lord God, almighty and everlasting Father, you have brought us in safety
to this new day: Preserve us with your mighty power, that we may not fall
into sin, nor be overcome by adversity; and in all we do, direct us to the
fulfilling of your purpose; through Jesus Christ our Lord. *Amen.*

Prayer for Mission

Lord Jesus Christ, you stretched out your arms of love on the hard wood
of the cross that everyone might come within the reach of your saving
embrace: So clothe us in your Spirit that we, reaching forth our hands in
love, may bring those who do not know you to the knowledge and love of
you; for the honor of your Name. *Amen.*

General Thanksgiving (said together)

Almighty God, Father of all mercies,
we your unworthy servants give you humble thanks
for all your goodness and loving-kindness
to us and to all whom you have made.
We bless you for our creation, preservation,
and all the blessings of this life;
but above all for your immeasurable love
in the redemption of the world by our Lord Jesus Christ;
for the means of grace, and for the hope of glory.
And, we pray, give us such an awareness of your mercies,
that with truly thankful hearts
we may show forth your praise,
not only with our lips, but in our lives,
by giving up our selves to your service,
and by walking before you
in holiness and righteousness all our days;
through Jesus Christ our Lord,
to whom, with you and the Holy Spirit,
be honor and glory throughout all ages. Amen.

Officiant	Let us bless the Lord.
All	**Thanks be to God.**

Officiant   † The grace of our Lord Jesus Christ, and the love of
God, and the fellowship of the Holy Spirit, be with us all
evermore. Amen.
2 Corinthians 13:14

Thursday
<u>Morning Prayer</u>

Officiant   † Lord, open our lips.

All   **And our mouth shall proclaim your praise.**

Officiant   † O God, make speed to save us.

All   **O Lord, make haste to help us.**

† Glory be to the Father, and to the Son, and to the Holy Spirit; as it was in the beginning, is now, and ever shall be; world without end. Amen.

Venite *O Come*
Psalm 95:1-8; 96:9,13

O come, let us sing to the Lord;
let us shout for joy to the Rock of our salvation.
Let us come before his presence with thanksgiving
and raise a loud shout to him with psalms.

For the Lord is a great God,
and a great King above all gods.
In his hand are the caverns of the earth,
and the heights of the hills are his also.

The sea is his, for he made it,
and his hands have molded the dry land.
O come, let us worship and bow down,
and kneel before the Lord our Maker.

For he is our God,
and we are the people of his pasture and the sheep of his hand.
Today, if you hear his voice,
Do not harden your heart, as in the rebellion.

O worship the Lord in the beauty of holiness;
let the whole earth stand in awe of him.
For he comes, for he comes to judge the earth
and with righteousness to judge the world
and the peoples in his faithfulness.

A Psalm Appointed for Thursdays
The following or some other psalm may be said.

Psalm 130

Out of the depths I cry to you, O LORD!
O LORD, hear my voice!
Let your ears be attentive to the voice of my supplication!

If you, O LORD, should mark iniquities,
O Lord, who could stand?

But with you there is forgiveness,
that you may be feared.

I wait for the LORD, my soul waits,
and in his word I put my hope;

My soul waits for the Lord
more than watchmen wait for the morning,
more than watchmen wait for the morning.

O Israel, hope in the LORD!
For with the LORD there is steadfast love,

With him there is plentiful redemption.
and he will redeem Israel from all his iniquities.

At the end of the Psalms is said
† Glory be to the Father, and to the Son, and to the Holy Spirit:
as it was in the beginning, is now, and ever shall be,
world without end. Amen.

The Lessons
One or two Lessons from Scripture may be read. The following Canticle
may be sung or said between or after the Lessons.

The Song of Zechariah
Benedictus Dominus Deus
Luke 1: 68-79

Blessed be the Lord, the God of Israel;
he has come to his people and set them free.

He has raised up for us a mighty savior,
born of the house of his servant David.

Through his holy prophets he promised of old,
that he would save us from our enemies,
from the hands of all who hate us.

He promised to show mercy to our fathers
and to remember his holy covenant.

This was the oath he swore to our father Abraham,
to set us free from the hands of our enemies,

Free to worship him without fear,
holy and righteous in his sight
all the days of our life.

You, my child, shall be called the prophet of the Most High,
for you will go before the Lord to prepare his way,

To give his people knowledge of salvation
by the forgiveness of their sins.

In the tender compassion of our God
the dawn from on high shall break upon us,

To shine on those who dwell in darkness
and the shadow of death,
and to guide our feet into the way of peace.

† Glory be to the Father, and to the Son, and to the Holy Spirit:
as it was in the beginning, is now, and ever shall be,
world without end. Amen.

The Creed

I believe in one God,
    the Father, the Almighty,
    maker of heaven and earth,
    of all that is, visible and invisible.

I believe in one Lord, Jesus Christ,
    the only-begotten Son of God,
    eternally begotten of the Father,
    God from God, Light from Light,
    true God from true God,
    begotten, not made,
    of one Being with the Father;
    through him all things were made.
For us and for our salvation he came down from heaven,
    was incarnate from the Holy Spirit and the Virgin Mary,
    and was made man.
For our sake he was crucified under Pontius Pilate;
    he suffered death and was buried.
On the third day he rose again in accordance with the Scriptures;
    he ascended into heaven
    and is seated at the right hand of the Father.
He will come again in glory to judge the living and the dead,
    and his kingdom will have no end.

I believe in the Holy Spirit, the Lord, the giver of life,
    who proceeds from the Father,
    who with the Father and the Son is worshiped and glorified,
    who has spoken through the prophets.
I believe in one holy catholic and apostolic Church.
I acknowledge one Baptism for the forgiveness of sins.
I look for the resurrection of the dead,
    † and the life of the world to come. Amen.

Officiant	Lord have mercy (upon us).
All	**Christ have mercy.** **Lord have mercy.**

Our Father, who art in heaven,
hallowed be thy Name,
thy kingdom come,
thy will be done,
on earth as it is in heaven.
Give us this day our daily bread.
And forgive us our trespasses,
as we forgive those
who trespass against us.
And lead us not into temptation,
but deliver us from evil.
For thine is the kingdom,
and the power, and the glory,
for ever and ever. Amen.

Officiant	God of all creation, full of love and abounding in mercy;
All	**May the whole earth be filled with your glory.**
Officiant	Lord, bless and guide all ministers of your church;
All	**Clothe them in righteousness and grant them wisdom.**
Officiant	Direct the leaders of our nation;
All	**That they may act in accordance with your kingdom.**
Officiant	Enlarge our own hearts, O Lord,
All	**To love the things that you love.**
Officiant	May we proclaim your light
All	**In every place where there is darkness.**

Officiant	May we proclaim your Holy Name
All	**In every aspect of our lives.**

Officiant	Create in us clean hearts, O God;
All	**And renew a right spirit within us.**

Officiant	Grant us your peace;
All	**For only in you can we live in safety.**

Officiant	We pray for those in sickness, grief, persecution, bondage, fear, and loneliness;
All	**Lord, have mercy.**

(pause to offer your own prayers or to sit in silence)

Collects
The Collect for the week may be said. Then,

Collect for Guidance

Heavenly Father, in you we live and move and have our being: We humbly pray you so to guide and govern us by your Holy Spirit, that in all the cares and occupations of our life we may not forget you, but may remember that we are ever walking in your sight; through Jesus Christ our Lord. *Amen.*

Prayer for Mission

O God, you have made of one blood all the peoples of the earth, and sent your blessed Son to preach peace to those who are far off and to those who are near: Grant that people everywhere may seek after you and find you; bring the nations into your fold; pour out your Spirit upon all flesh; and hasten the coming of your kingdom; through Jesus Christ our Lord. *Amen.*

General Thanksgiving (said together)

Almighty God, Father of all mercies,
we your unworthy servants give you humble thanks
for all your goodness and loving-kindness
to us and to all whom you have made.
We bless you for our creation, preservation,
and all the blessings of this life;
but above all for your immeasurable love
in the redemption of the world by our Lord Jesus Christ;
for the means of grace, and for the hope of glory.
And, we pray, give us such an awareness of your mercies,
that with truly thankful hearts
we may show forth your praise,
not only with our lips, but in our lives,
by giving up our selves to your service,
and by walking before you
in holiness and righteousness all our days;
through Jesus Christ our Lord,
to whom, with you and the Holy Spirit,
be honor and glory throughout all ages. Amen.

Officiant Let us bless the Lord.
All **Thanks be to God.**

Officiant † The grace of our Lord Jesus Christ, and the love of
God, and the fellowship of the Holy Spirit, be with us all
evermore. Amen.
2 Corinthians 13:14

Officiant	† Lord, open our lips.
All	**And our mouth shall proclaim your praise.**

Officiant	† O God, make speed to save us.
All	**O Lord, make haste to help us.**

† Glory be to the Father, and to the Son, and to the Holy Spirit; as it was in the beginning, is now, and ever shall be; world without end. Amen.

Venite *O Come*
Psalm 95:1-8; 96:9,13

O come, let us sing to the Lord;
let us shout for joy to the Rock of our salvation.
Let us come before his presence with thanksgiving
and raise a loud shout to him with psalms.

For the Lord is a great God,
and a great King above all gods.
In his hand are the caverns of the earth,
and the heights of the hills are his also.

The sea is his, for he made it,
and his hands have molded the dry land.
O come, let us worship and bow down,
and kneel before the Lord our Maker.

For he is our God,
and we are the people of his pasture and the sheep of his hand.
Today, if you hear his voice,
Do not harden your heart, as in the rebellion.

O worship the Lord in the beauty of holiness;
let the whole earth stand in awe of him.
For he comes, for he comes to judge the earth
and with righteousness to judge the world
and the peoples in his faithfulness.

A Psalm Appointed for Fridays
The following or some other psalm may be said.

Psalm 147:1-11

Praise the LORD!
How good it is to sing praises to our God;
for it is pleasant, and a song of praise is fitting.

The LORD builds up Jerusalem;
he gathers together the exiles of Israel.

He heals the brokenhearted
and binds up their wounds.

He determines the number of the stars;
he calls them each by name.

Great is our Lord and mighty in power;
his understanding is beyond all measure.

The LORD lifts up the humble;
but he casts the wicked to the ground.

Sing to the LORD with thanksgiving;
make melody to our God on the harp!

He covers the heavens with clouds,
preparing rain for the earth;
he makes the grass grow on the hillsides.

He provides food for the beasts,
and for the young ravens that cry.

His delight is not in the strength of the horse,
nor his pleasure in the legs of a man,

But the LORD delights in those who fear him,
in those who hope in his steadfast love.

At the end of the Psalms is said
† Glory be to the Father, and to the Son, and to the Holy Spirit:
as it was in the beginning, is now, and ever shall be,
world without end. Amen.

The Lessons
One or two Lessons from Scripture may be read. The following Canticle
may be sung or said between or after the Lessons.

A Song to the Lamb
Dignus es
Revelation 4:11; 5:9-10, 13

Splendor and honor and kingly power
are yours by right, O Lord our God,

For you created everything that is,
and by your will they were created and have their being;

And yours by right, O Lamb that was slain,
for with your blood you have redeemed for God,

From every family, language, people, and nation,
a kingdom of priests to serve our God.

And so, to him who sits upon the throne,
and to Christ the Lamb,

Be worship and praise, dominion and splendor,
for ever and for evermore.

The Creed

I believe in one God,
    the Father, the Almighty,
    maker of heaven and earth,
    of all that is, visible and invisible.

I believe in one Lord, Jesus Christ,
    the only-begotten Son of God,
    eternally begotten of the Father,
    God from God, Light from Light,
    true God from true God,
    begotten, not made,
    of one Being with the Father;
    through him all things were made.
For us and for our salvation he came down from heaven,
    was incarnate from the Holy Spirit and the Virgin Mary,
    and was made man.
For our sake he was crucified under Pontius Pilate;
    he suffered death and was buried.
On the third day he rose again in accordance with the Scriptures;
    he ascended into heaven
    and is seated at the right hand of the Father.
He will come again in glory to judge the living and the dead,
    and his kingdom will have no end.

I believe in the Holy Spirit, the Lord, the giver of life,
    who proceeds from the Father,
    who with the Father and the Son is worshiped and glorified,
    who has spoken through the prophets.
I believe in one holy catholic and apostolic Church.
I acknowledge one Baptism for the forgiveness of sins.
I look for the resurrection of the dead,
    † and the life of the world to come. Amen.

Officiant	Lord have mercy (upon us).
All	**Christ have mercy.**
	Lord have mercy.

Our Father, who art in heaven,
hallowed be thy Name,
thy kingdom come,
thy will be done,
on earth as it is in heaven.
Give us this day our daily bread.
And forgive us our trespasses,
as we forgive those
who trespass against us.
And lead us not into temptation,
but deliver us from evil.
For thine is the kingdom,
and the power, and the glory,
for ever and ever. Amen.

Officiant	God of all creation, full of love and abounding in mercy;
All	**May the whole earth be filled with your glory.**
Officiant	Lord, bless and guide all ministers of your church;
All	**Clothe them in righteousness and grant them wisdom.**
Officiant	Direct the leaders of our nation;
All	**That they may act in accordance with your kingdom.**
Officiant	Enlarge our own hearts, O Lord,
All	**To love the things that you love.**
Officiant	May we proclaim your light
All	**In every place where there is darkness.**

Officiant	May we proclaim your Holy Name
All	**In every aspect of our lives.**
Officiant	Create in us clean hearts, O God;
All	**And renew a right spirit within us.**
Officiant	Grant us your peace;
All	**For only in you can we live in safety.**
Officiant	We pray for those in sickness, grief, persecution, bondage, fear, and loneliness;
All	**Lord, have mercy.**

(pause to offer your own prayers or to sit in silence)

Collects
The Collect for the week may be said. Then,

Collect for Fridays

Almighty God, whose most dear Son went not up to joy but first he suffered pain, and entered not into glory before he was crucified: Mercifully grant that we, walking in the way of the cross, may find it none other than the way of life and peace; through Jesus Christ your Son our Lord. *Amen.*

Prayer for Mission

Almighty and everlasting God, by whose Spirit the whole body of your faithful people is governed and sanctified: Receive our supplications and prayers which we offer before you for all members of your holy Church, that in their vocation and ministry they may truly and devoutly serve you; through our Lord and Savior Jesus Christ. *Amen.*

General Thanksgiving (said together)

Almighty God, Father of all mercies,
we your unworthy servants give you humble thanks
for all your goodness and loving-kindness
to us and to all whom you have made.
We bless you for our creation, preservation,
and all the blessings of this life;
but above all for your immeasurable love
in the redemption of the world by our Lord Jesus Christ;
for the means of grace, and for the hope of glory.
And, we pray, give us such an awareness of your mercies,
that with truly thankful hearts
we may show forth your praise,
not only with our lips, but in our lives,
by giving up our selves to your service,
and by walking before you
in holiness and righteousness all our days;
through Jesus Christ our Lord,
to whom, with you and the Holy Spirit,
be honor and glory throughout all ages. Amen.

Officiant   Let us bless the Lord.
All   **Thanks be to God.**

Officiant   † The grace of our Lord Jesus Christ, and the love of
                       God, and the fellowship of the Holy Spirit, be with us all
                       evermore. Amen.
                       2 Corinthians 13:14

Officiant	† Lord, open our lips.
All	**And our mouth shall proclaim your praise.**
Officiant	† O God, make speed to save us.
All	**O Lord, make haste to help us.**

† Glory be to the Father, and to the Son, and to the Holy Spirit; as it was in the beginning, is now, and ever shall be; world without end. Amen.

Venite *O Come*
Psalm 95:1-8; 96:9,13

O come, let us sing to the Lord;
let us shout for joy to the Rock of our salvation.
Let us come before his presence with thanksgiving
and raise a loud shout to him with psalms.

For the Lord is a great God,
and a great King above all gods.
In his hand are the caverns of the earth,
and the heights of the hills are his also.

The sea is his, for he made it,
and his hands have molded the dry land.
O come, let us worship and bow down,
and kneel before the Lord our Maker.

For he is our God,
and we are the people of his pasture and the sheep of his hand.
Today, if you hear his voice,
Do not harden your heart, as in the rebellion.

O worship the Lord in the beauty of holiness;
let the whole earth stand in awe of him.
For he comes, for he comes to judge the earth
and with righteousness to judge the world
and the peoples in his faithfulness.

A Psalm Appointed for Saturdays
The following or some other psalm may be said.

Psalm 23

The LORD is my shepherd;
I shall not want.

He makes me lie down in green pastures;
he leads me beside still waters.

He restores my soul;
he leads me in paths of righteousness for his Name's sake.

Yea, though I walk through the valley of the shadow of death,
I will fear no evil,

For you are with me;
your rod and your staff, they comfort me.

You prepare a table before me in the presence of my enemies;
you anoint my head with oil; my cup overflows.

Surely goodness and mercy will follow me all the days of my life,
and I will dwell in the house of the LORD forever.

At the end of the Psalms is said
† Glory be to the Father, and to the Son, and to the Holy Spirit:
as it was in the beginning, is now, and ever shall be,
world without end. Amen.

The Lessons
One or two Lessons from Scripture may be read. The following Canticle may be sung or said between or after the Lessons.

The Song of Zechariah
Benedictus Dominus Deus
Luke 1: 68-79

Blessed be the Lord, the God of Israel;
he has come to his people and set them free.

He has raised up for us a mighty savior,
born of the house of his servant David.

Through his holy prophets he promised of old,
that he would save us from our enemies,
from the hands of all who hate us.

He promised to show mercy to our fathers
and to remember his holy covenant.

This was the oath he swore to our father Abraham,
to set us free from the hands of our enemies,

Free to worship him without fear,
holy and righteous in his sight
all the days of our life.

You, my child, shall be called the prophet of the Most High,
for you will go before the Lord to prepare his way,

To give his people knowledge of salvation
by the forgiveness of their sins.

In the tender compassion of our God
the dawn from on high shall break upon us,

To shine on those who dwell in darkness
and the shadow of death,
and to guide our feet into the way of peace.

† Glory be to the Father, and to the Son, and to the Holy Spirit:
as it was in the beginning, is now, and ever shall be,
world without end. Amen.

The Creed

I believe in one God,
>   the Father, the Almighty,
>   maker of heaven and earth,
>   of all that is, visible and invisible.

I believe in one Lord, Jesus Christ,
>   the only-begotten Son of God,
>   eternally begotten of the Father,
>   God from God, Light from Light,
>   true God from true God,
>   begotten, not made,
>   of one Being with the Father;
>   through him all things were made.
For us and for our salvation he came down from heaven,
>   was incarnate from the Holy Spirit and the Virgin Mary,
>   and was made man.
For our sake he was crucified under Pontius Pilate;
>   he suffered death and was buried.
On the third day he rose again in accordance with the Scriptures;
>   he ascended into heaven
>   and is seated at the right hand of the Father.
He will come again in glory to judge the living and the dead,
>   and his kingdom will have no end.

I believe in the Holy Spirit, the Lord, the giver of life,
>   who proceeds from the Father,
>   who with the Father and the Son is worshiped and glorified,
>   who has spoken through the prophets.
I believe in one holy catholic and apostolic Church.
I acknowledge one Baptism for the forgiveness of sins.
I look for the resurrection of the dead,
>   † and the life of the world to come. Amen.

Officiant　Lord have mercy (upon us).
All　**Christ have mercy.**
Lord have mercy.

Our Father, who art in heaven,
hallowed be thy Name,
thy kingdom come,
thy will be done,
on earth as it is in heaven.
Give us this day our daily bread.
And forgive us our trespasses,
as we forgive those
who trespass against us.
And lead us not into temptation,
but deliver us from evil.
For thine is the kingdom,
and the power, and the glory,
for ever and ever. Amen.

Officiant　God of all creation, full of love and abounding in mercy;
All　**May the whole earth be filled with your glory.**

Officiant　Lord, bless and guide all ministers of your church;
All　**Clothe them in righteousness and grant them wisdom.**

Officiant　Direct the leaders of our nation;
All　**That they may act in accordance with your kingdom.**

Officiant　Enlarge our own hearts, O Lord,
All　**To love the things that you love.**

Officiant　May we proclaim your light
All　**In every place where there is darkness.**

Officiant	May we proclaim your Holy Name
All	**In every aspect of our lives.**
Officiant	Create in us clean hearts, O God;
All	**And renew a right spirit within us.**
Officiant	Grant us your peace;
All	**For only in you can we live in safety.**
Officiant	We pray for those in sickness, grief, persecution, bondage, fear, and loneliness;
All	**Lord, have mercy.**

(pause to offer your own prayers or to sit in silence)

Collects
The Collect for the week may be said. Then,

Collect for Saturdays

Almighty God, who after the creation of the world rested from all your works and sanctified a day of rest for all your creatures: Grant that we, putting away all earthly anxieties, may be duly prepared for the service of your sanctuary, and that our rest here upon earth may be a preparation for the eternal rest promised to your people in heaven; through Jesus Christ our Lord. *Amen.*

Prayer for Mission

Lord Jesus Christ, you stretched out your arms of love on the hard wood of the cross that everyone might come within the reach of your saving embrace: So clothe us in your Spirit that we, reaching forth our hands in love, may bring those who do not know you to the knowledge and love of you; for the honor of your Name. *Amen.*

General Thanksgiving (said together)

Almighty God, Father of all mercies,
we your unworthy servants give you humble thanks
for all your goodness and loving-kindness
to us and to all whom you have made.
We bless you for our creation, preservation,
and all the blessings of this life;
but above all for your immeasurable love
in the redemption of the world by our Lord Jesus Christ;
for the means of grace, and for the hope of glory.
And, we pray, give us such an awareness of your mercies,
that with truly thankful hearts
we may show forth your praise,
not only with our lips, but in our lives,
by giving up our selves to your service,
and by walking before you
in holiness and righteousness all our days;
through Jesus Christ our Lord,
to whom, with you and the Holy Spirit,
be honor and glory throughout all ages. Amen.

Officiant	Let us bless the Lord.
All	**Thanks be to God.**

Officiant † The grace of our Lord Jesus Christ, and the love of God, and the fellowship of the Holy Spirit, be with us all evermore. Amen.
2 Corinthians 13:14

MID-DAY PRAYER

Officiant   O God, make speed to save us;

All   **O Lord, make haste to help us.**

Glory be to the Father, and to the Son, and to the Holy Spirit: as it was in the beginning, is now, and ever shall be, world without end. Amen.

One or more of the following Psalms may be said

Psalm 123

Unto you I lift up my eyes,
O you enthroned in the heavens!

Behold, as the eyes of servants look to the hand of their master,
as the eyes of a maid to the hand of her mistress,

So our eyes look to the LORD our God,
until he has mercy upon us.

Have mercy upon us, O LORD, have mercy:
for we are exceedingly filled with contempt.

Our soul is exceedingly filled
with the scorn of those who are at ease,
and with the contempt of the proud.

Psalm 22:22-31

I will tell of your Name to my brothers;
in the midst of the congregation I will praise you:

You who fear the LORD, praise him!
all you descendants of Jacob, glorify him;
stand in awe of him, all you offspring of Israel!

For he has not despised nor abhorred
the affliction of the afflicted,

And he has not hidden his face from him,
but has heard his cry for help.

From you comes my praise in the great congregation;
I will pay my vows before those who fear him.

The poor shall eat and be satisfied;
those who seek the LORD shall praise him!
May your hearts live forever!

All the ends of the earth shall remember
and turn to the LORD,
and all the families of the nations shall worship before you.

For the kingdom is the LORD's;
He rules over the nations.

All the prosperous of the earth will eat and worship;
before him shall bow all who go down to the dust —
those who cannot keep themselves alive.

Posterity shall serve him;
the coming generation will be told about the LORD;

They will proclaim his righteousness to a people yet unborn:
He has done it.

Psalm 33

Rejoice in the LORD, O you righteous!
It befits the upright to praise him.

Give thanks to the LORD with the lyre;
make music to him on the harp of ten strings!

Sing to him a new song;
play skillfully, with shouts of joy.

For the word of the LORD is right and true,
and all his works are faithfulness.

He loves righteousness and justice;
the earth is full of the goodness of the LORD.

By the word of the LORD the heavens were made;
by the breath of his mouth their starry host.

He gathers up the waters of the sea as a heap;
he puts the deeps into storehouses.

Let all the earth fear the LORD;
let all the inhabitants of the world stand in awe of him!

For he spoke, and it came to be;
he commanded, and it stood firm.

The LORD brings the counsel of the nations to nothing;
he frustrates the plans of the peoples.

The counsel of the LORD stands firm forever,
the plans of his heart through all generations.

Blessed is the nation whose God is the LORD,
the people he has chosen as his own inheritance!

The LORD looks down from the heavens;
he sees all the children of man;

From his dwelling place he looks upon
all the inhabitants of the earth,

He who fashions the hearts of them all
observes everything they do.

The king is not saved by the size of his army;
a warrior is not delivered by his great strength.

A horse is a false hope for salvation;
despite all its strength it cannot save.

Behold, the eye of the LORD is on those who fear him,
on those whose hope is in his mercy,

To deliver their soul from death
and to keep them alive in famine.

Our soul waits for the LORD;
he is our help and our shield.

For in him our heart shall rejoice,
because we trust in his holy Name.

Let your steadfast love, O LORD, be upon us,
even as we have our hope in you.

At the end of the Psalms is said
Glory be to the Father, and to the Son, and to the Holy Spirit:
as it was in the beginning, is now, and ever shall be,
world without end. Amen.

The following or some other passage of Scripture is read

Wash yourselves; make yourselves clean; remove the evil of your deeds
from before my eyes; cease to do evil, learn to do good; seek justice,
defend the oppressed; take up the cause of the fatherless; plead the case of
the widow. Come now, let us reason together, says the Lord: though your
sins are like scarlet, they shall be as white as snow; though they are red
like crimson, they shall become like wool. If you are willing and obedient,
you shall eat the good of the land; but if you refuse and rebel, you shall be
eaten by the sword; for the mouth of the Lord has spoken.   *Isaiah 1:16-20*

A brief silence is kept.

Work out your own salvation with fear and trembling, for it is God who
works in you, both to will and to work for his good pleasure.
Philippians 2:12b-13 ESV

A brief silence is kept.

If anyone is in Christ, he is a new creation; the old has passed away;
behold, the new has come. All this is from God, who through Christ
reconciled us to himself and gave us the ministry of reconciliation.
2 Corinthians 5:17-18

A brief silence is kept.

Officiant   Lord have mercy (upon us).

All   **Christ have mercy.**
Lord have mercy.

All   **Our Father, who art in heaven,
          hallowed be thy Name,
          thy kingdom come, thy will be done,
          on earth as it is in heaven.
          Give us this day our daily bread.
          And forgive us our trespasses,
          as we forgive those who trespass against us.
          And lead us not into temptation,
          but deliver us from evil.
          For thine is the kingdom, and the power,
          and the glory, for ever and ever. Amen.**

Officiant   Lord, hear our prayer.

All   **And let our cry come to you.**

Silence is kept and free intercessions or petitions may be offered

The Officiant concludes

Heavenly Father, send your Holy Spirit into our hearts, to direct and rule
us according to your will, to comfort us in all our afflictions, to defend us
from all error, and to lead us into all truth; through Jesus Christ our Lord.
Amen.

Officiant   Let us bless the Lord.

All   **Thanks be to God.**

Officiant   The grace of our Lord Jesus Christ, and the love of God,
                and the fellowship of the Holy Spirit, be with us all
                evermore. Amen.
                2 Corinthians 13:14

Officiant   O God, make speed to save us;

All   **O Lord, make haste to help us.**

Glory be to the Father, and to the Son, and to the Holy Spirit: as it was in the beginning, is now, and ever shall be, world without end. Amen.

One or more of the following Psalms may be said

Psalm 127

Unless the LORD builds the house,
those who build it labor in vain.

Unless the LORD watches over the city,
the watchman stays awake in vain.

It is in vain that you rise up early and go late to bed,
eating the bread of anxious toil;
for he gives sleep to his beloved.

Behold, children are a heritage from the LORD,
and the fruit of the womb is a reward.

Like arrows in the hand of a warrior,
so are the children of one's youth.

Blessed is the man whose quiver is filled with them!
He shall not be put to shame
when he contends with his enemies in the gate.

Psalm 92

It is good to give thanks to the LORD,
to sing praises to your Name, O Most High;

To proclaim your steadfast love in the morning,
and your faithfulness every night,

With the ten-stringed lute, with the harp,
and with the melody of the lyre.

For you, O LORD, have made me glad by what you have done;
I will sing for joy at the works of your hands.

How great are your works, O LORD!
How profound your thoughts!

The senseless man cannot know;
the fool cannot understand,

That though the wicked sprout like grass
and all evildoers flourish,

They shall be utterly destroyed forever;
but you, O LORD, are on high forevermore.

For behold, your enemies, O LORD,
for behold, your enemies shall perish;
and all evildoers shall be scattered.

You have exalted my horn like that of the wild ox;
you have anointed me with fresh oil.

My eyes have seen the downfall of my enemies;
my ears have heard the doom of my wicked foes.

The righteous will flourish like a palm tree;
he shall grow like a cedar in Lebanon.

Those who are planted in the house of the LORD;
shall flourish in the courts of our God.

They will still bear fruit in old age;
they are ever full of sap and very green,

To show that the LORD is upright;
he is my rock, in whom no fault can be found.

Psalm 19

The heavens declare the glory of God,
and the skies proclaim the work of his hands.

Day unto day pours forth speech,
and night unto night reveals knowledge.

There is no speech or language where their voice is not heard.
Their voice goes out through all the earth,
and their words to the ends of the world.

In the heavens he has set up a tent for the sun,
which comes forth like a bridegroom out of his chamber,
and, like a champion, rejoices to run his course.

His rising is from one end of the heavens,
and his circuit to the other;
there is nothing hidden from his heat.

The law of the LORD is perfect,
reviving the soul;

The testimony of the LORD is sure,
making wise the simple;

The precepts of the LORD are right,
rejoicing the heart;

The commandment of the LORD is pure,
enlightening the eyes;

The fear of the LORD is clean,
enduring forever;

The judgments of the LORD are true,
and altogether righteous.

They are more to be desired than gold, even much fine gold;
sweeter far than honey, than honey dripping from the comb.

By them is your servant warned;
in keeping them there is great reward.

Who can discern his own errors?
Cleanse me from my hidden faults.

Keep your servant also from presumptuous sins;
let them not have dominion over me!
Then shall I be blameless, innocent of great transgression.

May the words of my mouth and the meditation of my heart
be pleasing in your sight,
O LORD, my rock and my redeemer.

At the end of the Psalms is said
Glory be to the Father, and to the Son, and to the Holy Spirit:
as it was in the beginning, is now, and ever shall be,
world without end. Amen.

The following or some other passage of Scripture is read

———————

A voice says, "Cry out!" And I said, "What shall I cry?" All flesh is grass, and all its beauty is like the flower of the field. The grass withers, and the flower fades when the breath of the Lord blows upon it. Surely the people are grass. The grass withers, and the flower fades, but the word of our God stands forever.   *Isaiah 40:6-8*

A brief silence is kept.

Let the word of Christ dwell in you richly, as you teach and admonish one another with all wisdom through psalms, and hymns, and spiritual songs, singing to God with gratitude in your hearts. And whatever you do, in word or deed, do it all in the name of the Lord Jesus, giving thanks to God the Father through him.
Colossians 3:16-17

A brief silence is kept.

If I have the gift of prophecy and can fathom all mysteries and all knowledge, and if I have all faith, so as to move mountains, but do not have love, I am nothing. If I give all I possess to the poor, and if I deliver up my body to be burned, but do not have love, I gain nothing.
1 Corinthians 13:2-3

A brief silence is kept.

———————

Officiant	Lord have mercy (upon us).
All	**Christ have mercy.** **Lord have mercy.**

All **Our Father, who art in heaven,
hallowed be thy Name,
thy kingdom come, thy will be done,
on earth as it is in heaven.
Give us this day our daily bread.
And forgive us our trespasses,
as we forgive those who trespass against us.
And lead us not into temptation,
but deliver us from evil.
For thine is the kingdom, and the power,
and the glory, for ever and ever. Amen.**

Officiant Lord, hear our prayer.

All **And let our cry come to you.**

Silence is kept and free intercessions or petitions may be offered

The Officiant concludes

Heavenly Father, send your Holy Spirit into our hearts, to direct and rule us according to your will, to comfort us in all our afflictions, to defend us from all error, and to lead us into all truth; through Jesus Christ our Lord. *Amen.*

Officiant Let us bless the Lord.

All **Thanks be to God.**

Officiant The grace of our Lord Jesus Christ, and the love of God, and the fellowship of the Holy Spirit, be with us all evermore. Amen.
2 Corinthians 13:14

Wednesday
Mid-Day Prayer

Officiant   O God, make speed to save us;

All   **O Lord, make haste to help us.**

Glory be to the Father, and to the Son, and to the Holy Spirit: as it was in the beginning, is now, and ever shall be, world without end. Amen.

One or more of the following Psalms may be said

Psalm 131

O LORD, my heart is not haughty;
my eyes are not set too high;

I do not occupy myself with great matters
things too profound, too marvelous for me.

But I have calmed and quieted my soul,
like a weaned child with his mother;
like a weaned child is my soul within me.

O Israel, hope in the LORD
from this time forth and for evermore.

Psalm 16

Preserve me, O God,
for in you I take refuge.

I say to the LORD, "You are my Lord;
apart from you I have no good thing."

As for the saints who are in the land,
they are the excellent ones
in whom is all my delight.

The sorrows of those will be multiplied
who chase after other gods.

Their drink offerings of blood I will not offer,
nor take their names upon my lips.

O LORD, you are the portion of my inheritance and my cup;
it is you who make my lot secure.

The lines have fallen for me in pleasant places;
indeed, I have a beautiful inheritance.

I will bless the LORD who gives me counsel;
even in the night my heart instructs me.

I have set the LORD always before me;
because he is at my right hand, I will not be shaken.

Therefore my heart is glad and my whole being rejoices;
my flesh also will dwell secure.

For you will not abandon me to Sheol,
nor let your holy one see decay.

You make known to me the path of life;
in your presence there is fullness of joy;
at your right hand are pleasures forevermore.

Psalm 145

I will exalt you, my God and King,
and bless your Name for ever and ever.

Every day I will bless you
and praise your Name for ever and ever.

Great is the LORD, and greatly to be praised;
his greatness is unsearchable.

One generation shall commend your works to another;
they shall tell of your mighty acts.

I will meditate on the glorious splendor of your majesty,
and on all your wondrous works.

Men shall speak of the might of your awesome deeds,
and I will declare your greatness.

They shall pour forth the fame of the abundance of your goodness
and they shall joyfully sing of your righteousness.

The LORD is gracious and full of compassion,
slow to anger and abounding in love.

The LORD is good to all,
and his tender mercy is over all he has made.

All your works shall praise you, O LORD,
and all your saints shall bless you!

They shall speak of the glory of your kingdom
and tell of your power,

To make known to the children of man your mighty deeds,
and the glorious splendor of your kingdom.

Your kingdom is an everlasting kingdom;
your dominion endures throughout all generations.

The LORD is faithful in all his words
and gracious in all he does.

The LORD upholds all those who fall
and raises up all who are bowed down.

The eyes of all look to you,
and you give them their food in due season.

You open your hand
and satisfy the desire of every living thing.

The LORD is righteous in all his ways
and gracious in all he does.

The LORD is near to all who call upon him,
to all who call on him in truth.

He fulfills the desire of those who fear him;
he also hears their cries and saves them.

The LORD preserves all those who love him,
but all the wicked he will destroy.

My mouth shall speak the praise of the LORD,
and let all flesh bless his holy Name for ever and ever.

At the end of the Psalms is said
Glory be to the Father, and to the Son, and to the Holy Spirit:
as it was in the beginning, is now, and ever shall be,
world without end. Amen.

The following or some other passage of Scripture is read

They have no knowledge who carry about their wooden idols, and keep on praying to a god that cannot save. There is no other god besides me, a righteous God and a Savior; there is none besides me. "Turn to me and be saved, all you ends of the earth! For I am God, and there is no other. By myself I have sworn; the word has gone out from my mouth in righteousness, and shall not return, that to me every knee shall bow, every tongue shall swear allegiance.' *Isaiah 45:20b,21b-23*

A brief silence is kept.

For the grace of God has appeared, bringing salvation for all people, training us to renounce ungodliness and worldly desires, and to live self-controlled, upright, and godly lives in the present age, waiting for our blessed hope, the appearing of the glory of our great God and Savior Jesus Christ, who gave himself for us, that he might redeem us from all lawlessness and purify for himself a people for his own possession who are zealous for good works. *Titus 2:11-14*

A brief silence is kept.

Long ago, at many times and in many ways, God spoke to our fathers by the prophets, but in these last days he has spoken to us by his Son, whom he appointed the heir of all things, through whom also he created the world. He is the radiance of God's glory and the exact representation of his being, upholding the universe by the word of his power. *Hebrews 1:1-3a*

A brief silence is kept.

Officiant   Lord have mercy (upon us).

All   **Christ have mercy.**
                   Lord have mercy.

All   **Our Father, who art in heaven,**
hallowed be thy Name,
thy kingdom come, thy will be done,
on earth as it is in heaven.
Give us this day our daily bread.
And forgive us our trespasses,
as we forgive those who trespass against us.
And lead us not into temptation,
but deliver us from evil.
For thine is the kingdom, and the power,
and the glory, for ever and ever. Amen.

Officiant   Lord, hear our prayer.

All   **And let our cry come to you.**

Silence is kept and free intercessions or petitions may be offered

The Officiant concludes

Heavenly Father, send your Holy Spirit into our hearts, to direct and rule us according to your will, to comfort us in all our afflictions, to defend us from all error, and to lead us into all truth; through Jesus Christ our Lord. *Amen*.

Officiant   Let us bless the Lord.

All   **Thanks be to God.**

Officiant   The grace of our Lord Jesus Christ, and the love of God, and the fellowship of the Holy Spirit, be with us all evermore. Amen.
2 Corinthians 13:14

Thursday
Mid-Day Prayer

Officiant   O God, make speed to save us;

All   **O Lord, make haste to help us.**

**Glory be to the Father, and to the Son, and to the
Holy Spirit: as it was in the beginning, is now, and
ever shall be, world without end. Amen.**

One or more of the following Psalms may be said

Psalm 90

Lord, you have been our dwelling place
in every generation.

Before the mountains were brought forth,
before you had formed the earth and the world,
from everlasting to everlasting you are God.

You turn man back into dust
saying, "Return, O children of man!"

For a thousand years in your sight
are like the day that has just gone by,
or like a watch in the night.

You sweep them away like a flood;
they are as a dream,
like new grass growing in the morning:

In the morning it flourishes and is renewed;
by the evening it fades and withers away.

For we are consumed by your anger;
by your wrath we are dismayed.

You have set our iniquities before you,
our secret sins in the light of your presence.

For all our days pass away in your fury;
we bring our years to an end like a sigh.

The span of our days is seventy years,
eighty perhaps for those who are strong;

yet their sum is but toil and sorrow;
they are soon gone, and we fly away.

Who understands the power of your anger,
and your wrath as great as the fear that is due you?

So teach us to number our days
that we may gain a heart of wisdom.

Return, O Lord! How long will it be?
Have compassion on your servants!

Satisfy us in the morning with your faithful love,
that we may rejoice and be glad all our days.

Make us glad for as many days as you have afflicted us,
for as many years as we have seen evil.

Let your work be shown to your servants,
and your glory to their children.

Let the beauty of the Lord our God be upon us,
establish the work of our hands for us;
yes, establish the work of our hands!

Psalm 25

To you, O LORD, I lift up my soul.
O my God, in you I trust;

Let me not be put to shame;
let not my enemies triumph over me.

Indeed, none who wait for you shall be put to shame;
but shame will come to those who are treacherous without cause.

Show me your ways, O LORD;
teach me your paths.

Lead me in your truth and teach me,
for you are the God of my salvation;
for you do I wait all the day long.

Remember, O LORD, your tender mercies and your faithful love,
for they have been from of old.

Remember not the sins of my youth, nor my transgressions;
according to your faithful love remember me,
for the sake of your goodness, O LORD!

Good and upright is the LORD;
therefore he instructs sinners in the way.

He leads the humble in what is right,
he teaches the humble his way.

All the paths of the LORD are steadfast love and faithfulness
to those who keep his covenant and his testimonies.

For the sake of your Name, O LORD,
pardon my iniquity, for it is great.

Who is the man who fears the LORD?
Him will he instruct in the way he should choose.

His soul shall abide in prosperity,
and his offspring shall inherit the land.

The LORD confides in those who fear him;
he reveals to them his covenant.

My eyes are ever toward the LORD,
for he will free my feet from the net.

Turn to me and be gracious to me,
for I am lonely and afflicted.

The troubles of my heart are enlarged;
bring me out of my distresses.

Look upon my affliction and my pain,
and forgive me all my sin.

Consider how many are my foes,
and with what violent hatred they have hated me.

O guard my soul and deliver me!
Let me not be put to shame,
for I have taken refuge in you.

May integrity and uprightness protect me,
for I wait for you.

Redeem Israel, O God,
out of all his troubles.

At the end of the Psalms is said
Glory be to the Father, and to the Son, and to the Holy Spirit:
as it was in the beginning, is now, and ever shall be,
world without end. Amen.

The following or some other passage of Scripture is read

He has shown you, O man, what is good. And what does the Lord require of you but to act justly, to love mercy, and to walk humbly with your God? *Micah 6:8*

A brief silence is kept.

Do nothing out of selfish ambition or vain conceit, but in humility count others more significant than yourselves. Let each of you look not only to his own interests, but also to the interests of others. *Philippians 2:3-4*

A brief silence is kept.

By this we know love, that Jesus Christ laid down his life for us; and we ought to lay down our lives for our brothers and sisters. But if anyone has the world's goods, and sees his brother in need, yet closes his heart against him, how does God's love abide in him? Dear children, let us not love with words or speech but with action and in truth. *1 John 3:16-18*

A brief silence is kept.

Officiant   Lord have mercy (upon us).

All   **Christ have mercy.**
Lord have mercy.

All   **Our Father, who art in heaven,
hallowed be thy Name,
thy kingdom come, thy will be done,
on earth as it is in heaven.
Give us this day our daily bread.
And forgive us our trespasses,
as we forgive those who trespass against us.
And lead us not into temptation,
but deliver us from evil.
For thine is the kingdom, and the power,
and the glory, for ever and ever. Amen.**

Officiant   Lord, hear our prayer.

All   **And let our cry come to you.**

Silence is kept and free intercessions or petitions may be offered

The Officiant concludes

Heavenly Father, send your Holy Spirit into our hearts, to direct and rule us according to your will, to comfort us in all our afflictions, to defend us from all error, and to lead us into all truth; through Jesus Christ our Lord. *Amen.*

Officiant   Let us bless the Lord.

All   **Thanks be to God.**

Officiant   The grace of our Lord Jesus Christ, and the love of God, and the fellowship of the Holy Spirit, be with us all evermore. Amen.
2 Corinthians 13:14

Friday
Mid-Day Prayer

Officiant	O God, make speed to save us;
All	**O Lord, make haste to help us.**

Glory be to the Father, and to the Son, and to the Holy Spirit: as it was in the beginning, is now, and ever shall be, world without end. Amen.

One or more of the following Psalms may be said

Psalm 3

O LORD, how many are my foes!
How many there are who rise up against me!

How many there are who say of my soul,
"There is no help for him in his God."

But you, O LORD, are a shield around me;
my glory, and the lifter of my head.

I cry aloud to the LORD,
and he answers me from his holy hill.

I lay me down and sleep;
I wake again, for the LORD sustains me.

I will not fear the tens of thousands
who have set themselves against me on every side.

Rise up, O LORD; set me free, O my God;
for you have struck all my enemies on the cheekbone;
you have broken the teeth of the wicked.

Salvation belongs to the LORD.
Your blessing be on your people!

Psalm 24

The earth is the LORD's and all that is in it,
the world and those who dwell therein,

For he has founded it upon the seas
and established it upon the rivers.

Who shall ascend the hill of the LORD?
and who shall stand in his holy place?

He who has clean hands and a pure heart,
who does not lift up his soul to falsehood
and does not swear deceitfully.

He will receive blessing from the LORD
and righteousness from the God of his salvation.

Such is the generation of those who seek him,
who seek your face, O God of Jacob.

Lift up your heads, O gates;
be lifted up, O ancient doors,
that the King of glory may come in.

Who is this King of glory?
The LORD, strong and mighty,
the LORD, mighty in battle!

Lift up your heads, O gates;
lift them up, O ancient doors,
that the King of glory may come in.

Who is this King of glory?
The LORD of hosts,
he is the King of glory!

<u>Psalm 103</u>

Bless the LORD, O my soul,
and all that is within me, bless his holy name!

Bless the LORD, O my soul,
and forget not all his benefits,

who forgives all your iniquities,
who heals all your diseases,

who redeems your life from destruction,
who crowns you with steadfast love and tender mercy,

who satisfies you with good things
so that your youth is renewed like the eagle's.

The LORD works righteousness
and justice for all who are oppressed.

He made known his ways to Moses,
his acts to the children of Israel.

The LORD is merciful and gracious,
slow to anger and abounding in steadfast love.

He will not always chide,
nor will he keep his anger forever.

He has not dealt with us according to our sins,
nor repaid us according to our iniquities.

For as high as the heavens are above the earth,
so great is his steadfast love toward those who fear him;

as far as the east is from the west,
so far has he removed our transgressions from us.

As a father has compassion for his children,
so the LORD has compassion for those who fear him.

For he knows our frame;
he remembers that we are dust.

As for man, his days are like grass;
he flourishes like a flower of the field;

the wind passes over it and it is gone,
and its place remembers it no more.

But the steadfast love of the LORD is from everlasting to everlasting on
those who fear him,
and his righteousness to children's children,

to those who keep his covenant
and remember his commandments and do them.

The LORD has established his throne in the heavens,
and his kingdom rules over all.

Bless the LORD, O you his angels,
you mighty ones who do his bidding,
obeying the voice of his word!

Bless the LORD, all you his hosts,
his ministers, who do his will!

Bless the LORD, all his works,
in all places of his dominion.
Bless the LORD, O my soul!

At the end of the Psalms is said
Glory be to the Father, and to the Son, and to the Holy Spirit:
as it was in the beginning, is now, and ever shall be,
world without end. Amen.

The following or some other passage of Scripture is read

———————

Is not this the fast that I choose: to loose the bonds of wickedness, to undo the heavy burdens, to let the oppressed go free, and to break every yoke? Is it not to share your bread with the hungry, and bring the homeless poor into your house; when you see the naked, to cover him, and not to hide yourself from your own flesh? Then your light shall break forth like the dawn, and your healing shall spring up speedily; your righteousness shall go before you, and the glory of the Lord shall be your rear guard. Then you shall call, and the Lord will answer; you shall cry, and he will say, 'Here I am.' *Isaiah 58:6-9a*

A brief silence is kept.

For by grace you have been saved through faith. And this is not your own doing; it is the gift of God, not a result of works, so that no one may boast. For we are his workmanship, created in Christ Jesus for good works, which God prepared beforehand, that we should walk in them.
Ephesians 2:8-10 ESV

A brief silence is kept.

Behold what manner of love the Father has bestowed upon us, that we should be called children of God, and such we are! For this reason the world does not know us, because it did not know him. Beloved, we are God's children now; and what we will be has not yet been revealed, but we know that when he is revealed, we shall be like him, for we shall see him as he is. *1 John 3:1-2*

A brief silence is kept.

———————

Officiant	Lord have mercy (upon us).
All	**Christ have mercy.** **Lord have mercy.**

All

Our Father, who art in heaven,
hallowed be thy Name,
thy kingdom come, thy will be done,
on earth as it is in heaven.
Give us this day our daily bread.
And forgive us our trespasses,
as we forgive those who trespass against us.
And lead us not into temptation,
but deliver us from evil.
For thine is the kingdom, and the power,
and the glory, for ever and ever. Amen.

Officiant   Lord, hear our prayer.

All   **And let our cry come to you.**

Silence is kept and free intercessions or petitions may be offered

The Officiant concludes

Heavenly Father, send your Holy Spirit into our hearts, to direct and rule us according to your will, to comfort us in all our afflictions, to defend us from all error, and to lead us into all truth; through Jesus Christ our Lord. *Amen.*

Officiant   Let us bless the Lord.

All   **Thanks be to God.**

Officiant   The grace of our Lord Jesus Christ, and the love of God, and the fellowship of the Holy Spirit, be with us all evermore. Amen.
2 Corinthians 13:14

Officiant   O God, make speed to save us;

All   **O Lord, make haste to help us.**

                   **Glory be to the Father, and to the Son, and to the
                   Holy Spirit: as it was in the beginning, is now, and
                   ever shall be, world without end. Amen.**

One or more of the following Psalms may be said

Psalm 46

God is our refuge and strength,
an ever-present help in trouble.

Therefore we will not fear, though the earth be moved,
though the mountains slip into the heart of the sea,

Though its waters roar and foam,
though the mountains tremble at its surging.

There is a river whose streams make glad the city of God,
the holy habitation of the Most High.

God is in the midst of her; she will not be moved;
God will help her when morning dawns.

The nations rage, the kingdoms fall;
he lifts his voice, the earth melts.

The LORD of hosts is with us;
the God of Jacob is our fortress.

Come, behold the works of the LORD,
what desolations he has brought on the earth.

He makes wars to cease throughout the earth;
he breaks the bow and shatters the spear,
and burns the chariots with fire.

"Be still, and know that I am God;
I will be exalted among the nations,
I will be exalted in the earth!"

The LORD of hosts is with us;
the God of Jacob is our fortress.

Psalm 139

O LORD, you have searched me and known me!
You know my sitting down and my rising up;
you discern my thoughts from afar.

You search out my path and my resting-places
and are acquainted with all my ways.

Even before a word is on my tongue,
behold, O LORD, you know it altogether.

You hem me in, behind and before,
and lay your hand upon me.

Such knowledge is too wonderful for me;
it is high; I cannot attain it.

Where can I go from your Spirit?
where can I flee from your presence?

If I ascend to the heavens, you are there!
If I make my bed in Sheol, you are there!

If I rise on the wings of the morning,
if I dwell in the uttermost part of the sea,

even there your hand will lead me;
your right hand will hold me fast.

If I say, "Surely the darkness will hide me,
and the light around me turn to night,"

The darkness is not dark to you;
the night is bright as the day,
for darkness and light are both alike to you.

For you formed my inmost being;
you knit me together in my mother's womb
.

I will praise you, for I am fearfully and wonderfully made.
Wonderful are your works; and that my soul knows very well.

My frame was not hidden from you,
while I was being made in secret,
intricately woven in the depths of the earth.

Your eyes have seen my unformed body,
and in your book were written
all the days that were formed for me,
when as yet there was none of them.

How precious to me are your thoughts, O God!
How vast is the sum of them!

If I should count them, they would outnumber the grains of sand.
When I awake, I am still with you.

Oh, that you would slay the wicked, O God!
O men of blood, depart from me!

For they speak against you wickedly;
your enemies take your Name in vain!

Do I not hate those who hate you, O LORD?
and do I not loathe those who rise up against you?

I hate them with a perfect hatred;
they have become my enemies.

Search me, O God, and know my heart!
try me and know my anxious thoughts!

See if there be any grievous way in me,
and lead me in the way everlasting!

At the end of the Psalms is said
Glory be to the Father, and to the Son, and to the Holy Spirit:
as it was in the beginning, is now, and ever shall be,
world without end. Amen.

The following or some other passage of Scripture is read

From the rising of the sun to its setting my Name shall be great among the
nations, and in every place incense shall be offered to my Name, and a
pure offering; for my Name shall be great among the nations, says the
LORD of hosts. *Malachi 1:11*

A brief silence is kept.

I urge you, brothers and sisters, by the mercies of God, to present your
bodies as a living sacrifice, holy and acceptable to God, which is your
spiritual worship. Do not be conformed to this world, but be transformed
by the renewing of your mind, that by testing you may discern what is the
will of God, that which is good and acceptable and perfect. *Romans 12:1-2*

A brief silence is kept.

As obedient children, do not be conformed to the lusts of your former
ignorance, but just as he who called you is holy, you also be holy in all
your conduct. For you know that you were ransomed from the futile ways
inherited from your forefathers, not with perishable things such as silver
or gold, but with the precious blood of Christ. He indeed was foreknown
before the foundation of the world, but was revealed in these last times for
your sake. *1 Peter 1:14-15,18-20*

A brief silence is kept.

Officiant   Lord have mercy (upon us).

All   **Christ have mercy.
                     Lord have mercy.**

All

Our Father, who art in heaven,
hallowed be thy Name,
thy kingdom come, thy will be done,
on earth as it is in heaven.
Give us this day our daily bread.
And forgive us our trespasses,
as we forgive those who trespass against us.
And lead us not into temptation,
but deliver us from evil.
For thine is the kingdom, and the power,
and the glory, for ever and ever. Amen.

Officiant   Lord, hear our prayer.

All   **And let our cry come to you.**

Silence is kept and free intercessions or petitions may be offered

The Officiant concludes

Heavenly Father, send your Holy Spirit into our hearts, to direct and rule us according to your will, to comfort us in all our afflictions, to defend us from all error, and to lead us into all truth; through Jesus Christ our Lord. *Amen.*

Officiant   Let us bless the Lord.

All   **Thanks be to God.**

Officiant   The grace of our Lord Jesus Christ, and the love of God, and the fellowship of the Holy Spirit, be with us all evermore. Amen.
           2 Corinthians 13:14

EVENING PRAYER

Sunday
<u>Evening Prayer</u>

Officiant   † O God, make speed to save us.

All   **O Lord, make haste to help us.**

† Glory be to the Father, and to the Son, and to the Holy Spirit;
as it was in the beginning, is now, and ever shall be;
world without end. Amen.

Phos Hilaron
O Gladsome Light

O gladsome light of the holy glory
of the everliving Father in heaven,
O Jesus Christ, holy and blessed!

Now as we come to the setting of the sun,
and our eyes behold the vesper light,
we sing your praises, O God: Father, Son, and Holy Spirit.

You are worthy at all times to be praised by joyful voices,
O Son of God, Giver of Life,
and to be glorified through all the worlds.

A Psalm Appointed for Sundays
The following or some other psalm may be said.

Psalm 36:1-9

The transgression of the wicked speaks deep in his heart;
there is no fear of God before his eyes.

For he flatters himself in his own eyes
that his iniquity will not be found out and be hated.

The words of his mouth are wickedness and deceit;
he has ceased to act wisely and to do good.

He plots wickedness while on his bed;
he sets himself on a way that is not good;
he does not reject evil.

Your love, O LORD, reaches to the heavens,
your faithfulness to the clouds.

Your righteousness is like the mighty mountains;
your judgments like the great deep;

O LORD, you preserve both man and beast.
How precious is your steadfast love, O God!

The children of man take refuge
in the shadow of your wings.

They feast on the abundance of your house;
you give them drink from the river of your delights.

For with you is the fountain of life;
in your light we see light.

At the end of the Psalms is said
† Glory be to the Father, and to the Son, and to the Holy Spirit:
as it was in the beginning, is now, and ever shall be,
world without end. Amen.

The Lessons
One or two Lessons from Scripture may be read. The following Canticle may be sung or said between or after the Lessons.

Magnificat
The Song of Mary - Luke 1:46-55

My soul magnifies the Lord,
and my spirit rejoices in God my Savior;

For he has regarded
the lowliness of his handmaiden.

For behold, from now on,
all generations will call me blessed;

For he that is mighty has magnified me,
and holy is his Name.

His mercy is on those who fear him,
throughout all generations.

He has shown the strength of his arm;
he has scattered the proud in the imagination of their hearts.

He has brought down the mighty from their thrones,
and has exalted the humble and meek.

He has filled the hungry with good things,
and the rich he has sent empty away.

He, remembering his mercy,
has helped his servant Israel,

As he promised to our fathers,
Abraham and his seed for ever.

† Glory be to the Father, and to the Son, and to the Holy Spirit;
As it was in the beginning, is now, and ever shall be;
World without end. Amen.

The Creed

I believe in one God,
    the Father, the Almighty,
    maker of heaven and earth,
    of all that is, visible and invisible.

I believe in one Lord, Jesus Christ,
    the only-begotten Son of God,
    eternally begotten of the Father,
    God from God, Light from Light,
    true God from true God,
    begotten, not made,
    of one Being with the Father;
    through him all things were made.
For us and for our salvation he came down from heaven,
    was incarnate from the Holy Spirit and the Virgin Mary,
    and was made man.
For our sake he was crucified under Pontius Pilate;
    he suffered death and was buried.
On the third day he rose again in accordance with the Scriptures;
    he ascended into heaven
    and is seated at the right hand of the Father.
He will come again in glory to judge the living and the dead,
    and his kingdom will have no end.

I believe in the Holy Spirit, the Lord, the giver of life,
    who proceeds from the Father,
    who with the Father and the Son is worshiped and glorified,
    who has spoken through the prophets.
I believe in one holy catholic and apostolic Church.
I acknowledge one Baptism for the forgiveness of sins.
I look for the resurrection of the dead,
    † and the life of the world to come. Amen.

Officiant   Lord have mercy (upon us).

All   **Christ have mercy.**
                   Lord have mercy.

                   Our Father, who art in heaven,
                   hallowed be thy Name,
                   thy kingdom come,
                   thy will be done,
                   on earth as it is in heaven.
                   Give us this day our daily bread.
                   And forgive us our trespasses,
                   as we forgive those
                   who trespass against us.
                   And lead us not into temptation,
                   but deliver us from evil.
                   For thine is the kingdom,
                   and the power, and the glory,
                   for ever and ever. Amen.

Officiant   For the day that is past; that worry and every anxious fear
                   may be put away from us; and that Christ would be
                   glorified in all we have done, we pray to you O Lord.

All   **Lord, have mercy.**

Officiant   That this evening may be holy, good, and peaceful; that
                   the angels of the Lord our God would encamp around us;
                   and that our weary souls may find their rest in Christ our
                   Savior, we pray to you O Lord.

All   **Lord, have mercy.**

Officiant	Create in us clean hearts, O God;
All	**And renew a right spirit within us.**
Officiant	Grant us your peace;
All	**For only in you can we live in safety.**
Officiant	We pray for those in sickness, grief, persecution, bondage, fear, and loneliness.
All	**Lord, have mercy.**
Officiant	Let us offer our own prayers.

(pause to offer your own prayers or to sit in silence)

Collects
The Collect for the week may be said. Then,

Collect for Sundays

Lord God, whose Son our Savior Jesus Christ triumphed over the powers of death and prepared for us our place in the new Jerusalem: Grant that we, who have this day given thanks for his resurrection, may praise you in that City of which he is the light, and where he lives and reigns for ever and ever. *Amen.*

Prayer for Mission

O God and Father of all, whom the whole heavens adore: Let the whole earth also worship you, all nations obey you, all tongues confess and bless you, and men and women everywhere love you and serve you in peace; through Jesus Christ our Lord. *Amen.*

General Thanksgiving (said together)

Almighty God, Father of all mercies,
we your unworthy servants give you humble thanks
for all your goodness and loving-kindness
to us and to all whom you have made.
We bless you for our creation, preservation,
and all the blessings of this life;
but above all for your immeasurable love
in the redemption of the world by our Lord Jesus Christ;
for the means of grace, and for the hope of glory.
And, we pray, give us such an awareness of your mercies,
that with truly thankful hearts
we may show forth your praise,
not only with our lips, but in our lives,
by giving up our selves to your service,
and by walking before you
in holiness and righteousness all our days;
through Jesus Christ our Lord,
to whom, with you and the Holy Spirit,
be honor and glory throughout all ages. Amen.

Officiant   Let us bless the Lord.

All   **Thanks be to God.**

Officiant   The grace of our Lord Jesus Christ, and the love of God,
                and the fellowship of the Holy Spirit, be with us all
                evermore. Amen.
                2 Corinthians 13:14

Officiant　　　　† O God, make speed to save us.

All　　　　**O Lord, make haste to help us.**

† Glory be to the Father, and to the Son, and to the Holy Spirit: as it was in the beginning, is now, and ever shall be, world without end. Amen.

Phos Hilaron
O Gladsome Light

O gladsome light of the holy glory
of the everliving Father in heaven,
O Jesus Christ, holy and blessed!

Now as we come to the setting of the sun,
and our eyes behold the vesper light,
we sing your praises, O God: Father, Son, and Holy Spirit.

You are worthy at all times to be praised by joyful voices,
O Son of God, Giver of Life,
and to be glorified through all the worlds.

A Psalm Appointed for Mondays
The following or some other psalm may be said.

Psalm 34:1-10
I will bless the LORD at all times;
his praise shall ever be in my mouth.

My soul shall make its boast in the LORD;
let the humble hear of it and rejoice.

O magnify the LORD with me
and let us exalt his Name together!

I sought the LORD, and he answered me;
he delivered me from all my fears.

Those who look to him are radiant;
their faces shall not be ashamed.

This poor man cried, and the LORD heard him
and saved him out of all his troubles.

The angel of the LORD encamps around those who fear him,
and he delivers them.

O taste and see that the LORD is good!
blessed is the man who takes refuge in him!

O fear the LORD, you his saints,
for those who fear him lack for nothing!

The young lions suffer want and hunger;
but those who seek the LORD lack no good thing.

At the end of the Psalms is said
† Glory be to the Father, and to the Son, and to the Holy Spirit:
as it was in the beginning, is now, and ever shall be,
world without end. Amen.

The Lessons
One or two Lessons from Scripture may be read. The following Canticle
may be sung or said between or after the Lessons.

Magnificat
The Song of Mary - Luke 1:46-55

My soul magnifies the Lord,
and my spirit rejoices in God my Savior;

For he has regarded
the lowliness of his handmaiden.

For behold, from now on,
all generations will call me blessed;

For he that is mighty has magnified me,
and holy is his Name.

His mercy is on those who fear him,
throughout all generations.

He has shown the strength of his arm;
he has scattered the proud in the imagination of their hearts.

He has brought down the mighty from their thrones,
and has exalted the humble and meek.

He has filled the hungry with good things,
and the rich he has sent empty away.

He, remembering his mercy,
has helped his servant Israel,

As he promised to our fathers,
Abraham and his seed for ever.

† Glory be to the Father, and to the Son, and to the Holy Spirit;
As it was in the beginning, is now, and ever shall be;
World without end. Amen.

The Creed

I believe in one God,
    the Father, the Almighty,
    maker of heaven and earth,
    of all that is, visible and invisible.

I believe in one Lord, Jesus Christ,
    the only-begotten Son of God,
    eternally begotten of the Father,
    God from God, Light from Light,
    true God from true God,
    begotten, not made,
    of one Being with the Father;
    through him all things were made.
For us and for our salvation he came down from heaven,
    was incarnate from the Holy Spirit and the Virgin Mary,
    and was made man.
For our sake he was crucified under Pontius Pilate;
    he suffered death and was buried.
On the third day he rose again in accordance with the Scriptures;
    he ascended into heaven
    and is seated at the right hand of the Father.
He will come again in glory to judge the living and the dead,
    and his kingdom will have no end.

I believe in the Holy Spirit, the Lord, the giver of life,
    who proceeds from the Father,
    who with the Father and the Son is worshiped and glorified,
    who has spoken through the prophets.
I believe in one holy catholic and apostolic Church.
I acknowledge one Baptism for the forgiveness of sins.
I look for the resurrection of the dead,
    † and the life of the world to come. Amen.

Officiant   Lord have mercy (upon us).

All   **Christ have mercy.**
Lord have mercy.

Our Father, who art in heaven,
hallowed be thy Name,
thy kingdom come,
thy will be done,
on earth as it is in heaven.
Give us this day our daily bread.
And forgive us our trespasses,
as we forgive those
who trespass against us.
And lead us not into temptation,
but deliver us from evil.
For thine is the kingdom,
and the power, and the glory,
for ever and ever. Amen.

Officiant   For the day that is past; that worry and every anxious fear may be put away from us; and that Christ would be glorified in all we have done, we pray to you O Lord.

All   **Lord, have mercy.**

Officiant   That this evening may be holy, good, and peaceful; that the angels of the Lord our God would encamp around us; and that our weary souls may find their rest in Christ our Savior, we pray to you O Lord.

All   **Lord, have mercy.**

Officiant	Create in us clean hearts, O God;
All	**And renew a right spirit within us.**
Officiant	Grant us your peace;
All	**For only in you can we live in safety.**
Officiant	We pray for those in sickness, grief, persecution, bondage, fear, and loneliness.
All	**Lord, have mercy.**
Officiant	Let us offer our own prayers.

(pause to offer your own prayers or to sit in silence)

Collects
The Collect for the week may be said. Then,

Collect for Peace
Most holy God, the source of all good desires, all right judgments, and all just works: Give to us, your servants, that peace which the world cannot give, so that our hearts may be fixed on the doing of your will, and that we, being delivered from the fear of all enemies, may live in peace and quietness; through the mercies of Christ Jesus our Savior. *Amen.*

Prayer for Mission
Keep watch, dear Lord, with those who work, or watch, or weep this night, and give your angels charge over those who sleep. Tend the sick, Lord Christ; give rest to the weary, bless the dying, soothe the suffering, pity the afflicted, shield the joyous; and all for your love's sake. *Amen.*

General Thanksgiving (said together)

Almighty God, Father of all mercies,
we your unworthy servants give you humble thanks
for all your goodness and loving-kindness
to us and to all whom you have made.
We bless you for our creation, preservation,
and all the blessings of this life;
but above all for your immeasurable love
in the redemption of the world by our Lord Jesus Christ;
for the means of grace, and for the hope of glory.
And, we pray, give us such an awareness of your mercies,
that with truly thankful hearts
we may show forth your praise,
not only with our lips, but in our lives,
by giving up our selves to your service,
and by walking before you
in holiness and righteousness all our days;
through Jesus Christ our Lord,
to whom, with you and the Holy Spirit,
be honor and glory throughout all ages. Amen.

Officiant　　Let us bless the Lord.

All　　**Thanks be to God.**

Officiant　　† The grace of our Lord Jesus Christ, and the love of
God, and the fellowship of the Holy Spirit, be with us all
evermore. Amen.
2 Corinthians 13:14

Officiant   † O God, make speed to save us.

All   **O Lord, make haste to help us.**

     † Glory be to the Father, and to the Son, and to the Holy Spirit: as it was in the beginning, is now, and ever shall be, world without end. Amen.

Phos Hilaron
O Gladsome Light

O gladsome light of the holy glory
of the everliving Father in heaven,
O Jesus Christ, holy and blessed!

Now as we come to the setting of the sun,
and our eyes behold the vesper light,
we sing your praises, O God: Father, Son, and Holy Spirit.

You are worthy at all times to be praised by joyful voices,
O Son of God, Giver of Life,
and to be glorified through all the worlds.

A Psalm Appointed for Tuesdays
The following or some other psalm may be said.

Psalm 30

I will extol you, O LORD, for you have lifted me up,
and have not let my enemies rejoice over me.

O LORD my God, I cried out to you for help,
and you have healed me.

O LORD, you have brought up my soul from Sheol;
you restored me to life, that I should not go down to the pit.

Sing praise to the LORD, O you his saints,
and give thanks to his holy name.

For his anger is but for a moment;
his favor is for a lifetime.

Weeping may remain for the night,
but joy comes in the morning.

As for me, I said in my prosperity,
"I shall never be moved."

By your favor, O LORD, you made my mountain stand strong;
but when you hid your face, I was filled with fear.

To you, O LORD, I cried out;
to the Lord I made my supplication:

"What profit is there in my destruction, if I go down to the pit?
Will the dust praise you? Will it declare your faithfulness?

Hear, O LORD, and be merciful to me!
O LORD, be my helper!"

You have turned my mourning into dancing;
you have removed my sackcloth and girded me with gladness,

So that my soul may sing your praise and not be silent.
O LORD my God, I will give you thanks forever!

At the end of the Psalms is said
† Glory be to the Father, and to the Son, and to the Holy Spirit:
as it was in the beginning, is now, and ever shall be,
world without end. Amen.

The Lessons

One or two Lessons from Scripture may be read. The following Canticle may be sung or said between or after the Lessons.

Magnificat
The Song of Mary - Luke 1:46-55

My soul magnifies the Lord,
and my spirit rejoices in God my Savior;

For he has regarded
the lowliness of his handmaiden.

For behold, from now on,
all generations will call me blessed;

For he that is mighty has magnified me,
and holy is his Name.

His mercy is on those who fear him,
throughout all generations.

He has shown the strength of his arm;
he has scattered the proud in the imagination of their hearts.

He has brought down the mighty from their thrones,
and has exalted the humble and meek.

He has filled the hungry with good things,
and the rich he has sent empty away.

He, remembering his mercy,
has helped his servant Israel,

As he promised to our fathers,
Abraham and his seed for ever.

† Glory be to the Father, and to the Son, and to the Holy Spirit;
As it was in the beginning, is now, and ever shall be;
World without end. Amen.

The Creed

I believe in one God,
>the Father, the Almighty,
>maker of heaven and earth,
>of all that is, visible and invisible.

I believe in one Lord, Jesus Christ,
>the only-begotten Son of God,
>eternally begotten of the Father,
>God from God, Light from Light,
>true God from true God,
>begotten, not made,
>of one Being with the Father;
>through him all things were made.
For us and for our salvation he came down from heaven,
>was incarnate from the Holy Spirit and the Virgin Mary,
>and was made man.
For our sake he was crucified under Pontius Pilate;
>he suffered death and was buried.
On the third day he rose again in accordance with the Scriptures;
>he ascended into heaven
>and is seated at the right hand of the Father.
He will come again in glory to judge the living and the dead,
>and his kingdom will have no end.

I believe in the Holy Spirit, the Lord, the giver of life,
>who proceeds from the Father,
>who with the Father and the Son is worshiped and glorified,
>who has spoken through the prophets.
I believe in one holy catholic and apostolic Church.
I acknowledge one Baptism for the forgiveness of sins.
I look for the resurrection of the dead,
>† and the life of the world to come. Amen.

Officiant   Lord have mercy (upon us).

All   **Christ have mercy.**
                  Lord have mercy.

                  Our Father, who art in heaven,
                  hallowed be thy Name,
                  thy kingdom come,
                  thy will be done,
                  on earth as it is in heaven.
                  Give us this day our daily bread.
                  And forgive us our trespasses,
                  as we forgive those
                  who trespass against us.
                  And lead us not into temptation,
                  but deliver us from evil.
                  For thine is the kingdom,
                  and the power, and the glory,
                  for ever and ever. Amen.

Officiant   For the day that is past; that worry and every anxious fear
                  may be put away from us; and that Christ would be
                  glorified in all we have done, we pray to you O Lord.

All   **Lord, have mercy.**

Officiant   That this evening may be holy, good, and peaceful; that
                  the angels of the Lord our God would encamp around us;
                  and that our weary souls may find their rest in Christ our
                  Savior, we pray to you O Lord.

All   **Lord, have mercy.**

Officiant	Create in us clean hearts, O God;
All	**And renew a right spirit within us.**
Officiant	Grant us your peace;
All	**For only in you can we live in safety.**
Officiant	We pray for those in sickness, grief, persecution, bondage, fear, and loneliness.
All	**Lord, have mercy.**
Officiant	Let us offer our own prayers.

(pause to offer your own prayers or to sit in silence)

Collects
The Collect for the week may be said. Then,

Collect for Aid Against Perils

Be our light in the darkness, O Lord, and in your great mercy defend us from all perils and dangers of this night; for the love of your only Son, our Savior Jesus Christ. *Amen.*

Prayer for Mission

O God, you manifest in your servants the signs of your presence: Send forth upon us the Spirit of love, that in companionship with one another your abounding grace may increase among us; through Jesus Christ our Lord. *Amen.*

General Thanksgiving (said together)

Almighty God, Father of all mercies,
we your unworthy servants give you humble thanks
for all your goodness and loving-kindness
to us and to all whom you have made.
We bless you for our creation, preservation,
and all the blessings of this life;
but above all for your immeasurable love
in the redemption of the world by our Lord Jesus Christ;
for the means of grace, and for the hope of glory.
And, we pray, give us such an awareness of your mercies,
that with truly thankful hearts
we may show forth your praise,
not only with our lips, but in our lives,
by giving up our selves to your service,
and by walking before you
in holiness and righteousness all our days;
through Jesus Christ our Lord,
to whom, with you and the Holy Spirit,
be honor and glory throughout all ages. Amen.

Officiant   Let us bless the Lord.

All   **Thanks be to God.**

Officiant   † The grace of our Lord Jesus Christ, and the love of
God, and the fellowship of the Holy Spirit, be with us all
evermore. Amen.
2 Corinthians 13:14

Wednesday
Evening Prayer

Officiant   † O God, make speed to save us.

All   **O Lord, make haste to help us.**

† Glory be to the Father, and to the Son, and to the Holy Spirit: as it was in the beginning, is now, and ever shall be, world without end. Amen.

Phos Hilaron
O Gladsome Light

O gladsome light of the holy glory
of the everliving Father in heaven,
O Jesus Christ, holy and blessed!

Now as we come to the setting of the sun,
and our eyes behold the vesper light,
we sing your praises, O God: Father, Son, and Holy Spirit.

You are worthy at all times to be praised by joyful voices,
O Son of God, Giver of Life,
and to be glorified through all the worlds.

A Psalm Appointed for Wednesdays
The following or some other psalm may be said.

Psalm 84

How lovely is your dwelling place,
O LORD Almighty!

My soul longs, yes, even faints
for the courts of the LORD;

My heart and flesh cry out
for the living God.

Even the sparrow has found a home,
and the swallow a nest for herself,
where she may lay her young,
at your altars, O LORD of hosts,
my King and my God.

Blessed are those who dwell in your house,
they are ever singing your praise!

Blessed are those whose strength is in you,
whose hearts are set on pilgrimage.

As they pass through the Valley of Weeping
they make it a place of springs;
yes, the early rain also covers it with pools.

They go from strength to strength;
and the God of gods will be seen in Zion.

O LORD God of hosts, hear my prayer;
give ear, O God of Jacob!

Behold our shield, O God;
look upon the face of your anointed!

For one day in your courts
is better than a thousand elsewhere.

I would rather be a doorkeeper in the house of my God
than to dwell in the tents of wickedness.

For the LORD God is a sun and shield;
the LORD bestows favor and honor.

No good thing does he withhold
from those who walk uprightly.

O LORD of hosts,
blessed is the one who trusts in you!

At the end of the Psalms is said
† Glory be to the Father, and to the Son, and to the Holy Spirit:
as it was in the beginning, is now, and ever shall be,
world without end. Amen.

The Lessons
One or two Lessons from Scripture may be read. The following Canticle may be sung or said between or after the Lessons.

Magnificat
The Song of Mary - Luke 1:46-55

My soul magnifies the Lord,
and my spirit rejoices in God my Savior;

For he has regarded
the lowliness of his handmaiden.

For behold, from now on,
all generations will call me blessed;

For he that is mighty has magnified me,
and holy is his Name.

His mercy is on those who fear him,
throughout all generations.

He has shown the strength of his arm;
he has scattered the proud in the imagination of their hearts.

He has brought down the mighty from their thrones,
and has exalted the humble and meek.

He has filled the hungry with good things,
and the rich he has sent empty away.

He, remembering his mercy,
has helped his servant Israel,

As he promised to our fathers,
Abraham and his seed for ever.

† Glory be to the Father, and to the Son, and to the Holy Spirit;
As it was in the beginning, is now, and ever shall be;
World without end. Amen.

The Creed

I believe in one God,
 the Father, the Almighty,
 maker of heaven and earth,
 of all that is, visible and invisible.

I believe in one Lord, Jesus Christ,
 the only-begotten Son of God,
 eternally begotten of the Father,
 God from God, Light from Light,
 true God from true God,
 begotten, not made,
 of one Being with the Father;
 through him all things were made.
For us and for our salvation he came down from heaven,
 was incarnate from the Holy Spirit and the Virgin Mary,
 and was made man.
For our sake he was crucified under Pontius Pilate;
 he suffered death and was buried.
On the third day he rose again in accordance with the Scriptures;
 he ascended into heaven
 and is seated at the right hand of the Father.
He will come again in glory to judge the living and the dead,
 and his kingdom will have no end.

I believe in the Holy Spirit, the Lord, the giver of life,
 who proceeds from the Father,
 who with the Father and the Son is worshiped and glorified,
 who has spoken through the prophets.
I believe in one holy catholic and apostolic Church.
I acknowledge one Baptism for the forgiveness of sins.
I look for the resurrection of the dead,
 † and the life of the world to come. Amen.

Officiant   Lord have mercy (upon us).

All   **Christ have mercy.**
                Lord have mercy.

                Our Father, who art in heaven,
                hallowed be thy Name,
                thy kingdom come,
                thy will be done,
                on earth as it is in heaven.
                Give us this day our daily bread.
                And forgive us our trespasses,
                as we forgive those
                who trespass against us.
                And lead us not into temptation,
                but deliver us from evil.
                For thine is the kingdom,
                and the power, and the glory,
                for ever and ever. Amen.

Officiant   For the day that is past; that worry and every anxious fear
                may be put away from us; and that Christ would be
                glorified in all we have done, we pray to you O Lord.

All   **Lord, have mercy.**

Officiant   That this evening may be holy, good, and peaceful; that
                the angels of the Lord our God would encamp around us;
                and that our weary souls may find their rest in Christ our
                Savior, we pray to you O Lord.

All   **Lord, have mercy.**

Officiant	Create in us clean hearts, O God;
All	**And renew a right spirit within us.**
Officiant	Grant us your peace;
All	**For only in you can we live in safety.**
Officiant	We pray for those in sickness, grief, persecution, bondage, fear, and loneliness.
All	**Lord, have mercy.**
Officiant	Let us offer our own prayers.

(pause to offer your own prayers or to sit in silence)

Collects
The Collect for the week may be said. Then,

Collect for Protection

O God, the life of all who live, the light of the faithful, the strength of those who labor, and the repose of the dead: We thank you for the blessings of the day that is past, and humbly ask for your protection through the coming night. Bring us in safety to the morning hours; through him who died and rose again for us, your Son our Savior Jesus Christ. *Amen.*

Prayer for Mission

O God and Father of all, whom the whole heavens adore: Let the whole earth also worship you, all nations obey you, all tongues confess and bless you, and men and women everywhere love you and serve you in peace; through Jesus Christ our Lord. *Amen.*

General Thanksgiving (said together)

Almighty God, Father of all mercies,
we your unworthy servants give you humble thanks
for all your goodness and loving-kindness
to us and to all whom you have made.
We bless you for our creation, preservation,
and all the blessings of this life;
but above all for your immeasurable love
in the redemption of the world by our Lord Jesus Christ;
for the means of grace, and for the hope of glory.
And, we pray, give us such an awareness of your mercies,
that with truly thankful hearts
we may show forth your praise,
not only with our lips, but in our lives,
by giving up our selves to your service,
and by walking before you
in holiness and righteousness all our days;
through Jesus Christ our Lord,
to whom, with you and the Holy Spirit,
be honor and glory throughout all ages. Amen.

Officiant	Let us bless the Lord.
All	**Thanks be to God.**
Officiant	† The grace of our Lord Jesus Christ, and the love of God, and the fellowship of the Holy Spirit, be with us all evermore. Amen. *2 Corinthians 13:14*

Officiant   † O God, make speed to save us.

All   **O Lord, make haste to help us.**

† Glory be to the Father, and to the Son, and to the Holy Spirit; as it was in the beginning, is now, and ever shall be; world without end. Amen.

Phos Hilaron
O Gladsome Light

O gladsome light of the holy glory
of the everliving Father in heaven,
O Jesus Christ, holy and blessed!

Now as we come to the setting of the sun,
and our eyes behold the vesper light,
we sing your praises, O God: Father, Son, and Holy Spirit.

You are worthy at all times to be praised by joyful voices,
O Son of God, Giver of Life,
and to be glorified through all the worlds.

A Psalm Appointed for Thursdays
The following or some other psalm may be said.
Psalm 143

Hear my prayer, O LORD; give ear to my cry for mercy!
In your faithfulness answer me, in your righteousness!

Enter not into judgment with your servant,
for no one living is righteous before you.

For the enemy has pursued my soul;
he has crushed my life to the ground;

he has made me to dwell in dark places
like those long dead.

So my spirit grows faint within me;
my heart within me is desolate.

I remember the days of old; I meditate on all you have done;
I ponder the work of your hands.

I stretch out my hands to you;
my soul thirsts for you like a parched land.

Answer me quickly, O LORD!
My spirit fails!

Hide not your face from me,
lest I become like those who go down to the pit.

Let the morning bring me word of your steadfast love,
for I put my trust in you.

Show me the way I should go,
for to you I lift up my soul.

Deliver me, O LORD, from my enemies
for I flee to you for refuge.

Teach me to do your will, for you are my God!
Let your good Spirit lead me on level ground!

For the sake of your Name, O LORD, preserve my life;
in your righteousness bring my soul out of trouble!

In your steadfast love, silence my enemies;
destroy all the adversaries of my soul,
for I am your servant.

At the end of the Psalms is said
† Glory be to the Father, and to the Son, and to the Holy Spirit:
as it was in the beginning, is now, and ever shall be,
world without end. Amen.

The Lessons

One or two Lessons from Scripture may be read. The following Canticle may be sung or said between or after the Lessons.

Magnificat
The Song of Mary - Luke 1:46-55

My soul magnifies the Lord,
and my spirit rejoices in God my Savior;

For he has regarded
the lowliness of his handmaiden.

For behold, from now on,
all generations will call me blessed;

For he that is mighty has magnified me,
and holy is his Name.

His mercy is on those who fear him,
throughout all generations.

He has shown the strength of his arm;
he has scattered the proud in the imagination of their hearts.

He has brought down the mighty from their thrones,
and has exalted the humble and meek.

He has filled the hungry with good things,
and the rich he has sent empty away.

He, remembering his mercy,
has helped his servant Israel,

As he promised to our fathers,
Abraham and his seed for ever.

† Glory be to the Father, and to the Son, and to the Holy Spirit;
As it was in the beginning, is now, and ever shall be;
World without end. Amen.

The Creed

I believe in one God,
 the Father, the Almighty,
 maker of heaven and earth,
 of all that is, visible and invisible.

I believe in one Lord, Jesus Christ,
 the only-begotten Son of God,
 eternally begotten of the Father,
 God from God, Light from Light,
 true God from true God,
 begotten, not made,
 of one Being with the Father;
 through him all things were made.
For us and for our salvation he came down from heaven,
 was incarnate from the Holy Spirit and the Virgin Mary,
 and was made man.
For our sake he was crucified under Pontius Pilate;
 he suffered death and was buried.
On the third day he rose again in accordance with the Scriptures;
 he ascended into heaven
 and is seated at the right hand of the Father.
He will come again in glory to judge the living and the dead,
 and his kingdom will have no end.

I believe in the Holy Spirit, the Lord, the giver of life,
 who proceeds from the Father,
 who with the Father and the Son is worshiped and glorified,
 who has spoken through the prophets.
I believe in one holy catholic and apostolic Church.
I acknowledge one Baptism for the forgiveness of sins.
I look for the resurrection of the dead,
 † and the life of the world to come. Amen.

Officiant   Lord have mercy (upon us).

All   **Christ have mercy.**
Lord have mercy.

Our Father, who art in heaven,
hallowed be thy Name,
thy kingdom come,
thy will be done,
on earth as it is in heaven.
Give us this day our daily bread.
And forgive us our trespasses,
as we forgive those
who trespass against us.
And lead us not into temptation,
but deliver us from evil.
For thine is the kingdom,
and the power, and the glory,
for ever and ever. Amen.

Officiant   For the day that is past; that worry and every anxious fear may be put away from us; and that Christ would be glorified in all we have done, we pray to you O Lord.

All   **Lord, have mercy.**

Officiant   That this evening may be holy, good, and peaceful; that the angels of the Lord our God would encamp around us; and that our weary souls may find their rest in Christ our Savior, we pray to you O Lord.

All   **Lord, have mercy.**

Officiant	Create in us clean hearts, O God;
All	**And renew a right spirit within us.**
Officiant	Grant us your peace;
All	**For only in you can we live in safety.**
Officiant	We pray for those in sickness, grief, persecution, bondage, fear, and loneliness.
All	**Lord, have mercy.**
Officiant	Let us offer our own prayers.

(pause to offer your own prayers or to sit in silence)

Collects
The Collect for the week may be said. Then,

Collect for the Presence of Christ

Lord Jesus, stay with us, for evening is at hand and the day is past; be our companion in the way, kindle our hearts, and awaken hope, that we may know you as you are revealed in Scripture and the breaking of bread. Grant this for the sake of your love. *Amen.*

Prayer for Mission

Keep watch, dear Lord, with those who work, or watch, or weep this night, and give your angels charge over those who sleep. Tend the sick, Lord Christ; give rest to the weary, bless the dying, soothe the suffering, pity the afflicted, shield the joyous; and all for your love's sake. *Amen.*

General Thanksgiving (said together)

Almighty God, Father of all mercies,
we your unworthy servants give you humble thanks
for all your goodness and loving-kindness
to us and to all whom you have made.
We bless you for our creation, preservation,
and all the blessings of this life;
but above all for your immeasurable love
in the redemption of the world by our Lord Jesus Christ;
for the means of grace, and for the hope of glory.
And, we pray, give us such an awareness of your mercies,
that with truly thankful hearts
we may show forth your praise,
not only with our lips, but in our lives,
by giving up our selves to your service,
and by walking before you
in holiness and righteousness all our days;
through Jesus Christ our Lord,
to whom, with you and the Holy Spirit,
be honor and glory throughout all ages. Amen.

Officiant   Let us bless the Lord.

All   **Thanks be to God.**

Officiant   † The grace of our Lord Jesus Christ, and the love of
God, and the fellowship of the Holy Spirit, be with us all
evermore. Amen.
2 Corinthians 13:14

Officiant   † O God, make speed to save us.

All   **O Lord, make haste to help us.**

† Glory be to the Father, and to the Son, and to the Holy Spirit: as it was in the beginning, is now, and ever shall be, world without end. Amen.

Phos Hilaron
O Gladsome Light

O gladsome light of the holy glory
of the everliving Father in heaven,
O Jesus Christ, holy and blessed!

Now as we come to the setting of the sun,
and our eyes behold the vesper light,
we sing your praises, O God: Father, Son, and Holy Spirit.

You are worthy at all times to be praised by joyful voices,
O Son of God, Giver of Life,
and to be glorified through all the worlds.

A Psalm Appointed for Fridays
The following or some other psalm may be said.

<u>Psalm 5</u>

Give ear to my words, O LORD;
consider my sighing.

Give heed to the voice of my cry, my King and my God,
for to you do I pray.

In the morning, LORD, you hear my voice;
in the morning I will lay my requests before you
and eagerly wait.

For you are not a God who delights in evil;
with you the wicked cannot dwell.

Braggarts cannot stand before your eyes;
you hate all workers of wickedness.

You destroy those who speak lies;
the LORD abhors the bloodthirsty and deceitful man.

But as for me, in the multitude of your mercy
I will come into your house;
I will bow down toward your holy temple in the fear of you.

Lead me, O LORD, in your righteousness because of my enemies;
make your way straight before my face.

For there is no truth in their mouth;
their inmost part is destruction itself;

Their throat is an open grave;
with their tongue they speak deceit.

Make them bear their guilt, O God;
let them fall by their own counsels.

Thrust them out because of the abundance of their transgressions,
for they have rebelled against you.

But let all who take refuge in you rejoice;
let them ever sing for joy.

Spread your protection over them,
that those who love your Name may exult in you.

For surely, LORD, you bless the righteous;
you surround him with favor as with a shield.

At the end of the Psalms is said
† Glory be to the Father, and to the Son, and to the Holy Spirit:
as it was in the beginning, is now, and ever shall be,
world without end. Amen.

The Lessons
One or two Lessons from Scripture may be read. The following Canticle may be sung or said between or after the Lessons.

Magnificat
The Song of Mary - Luke 1:46-55

My soul magnifies the Lord,
and my spirit rejoices in God my Savior;

For he has regarded
the lowliness of his handmaiden.

For behold, from now on,
all generations will call me blessed;

For he that is mighty has magnified me,
and holy is his Name.

His mercy is on those who fear him,
throughout all generations.

He has shown the strength of his arm;
he has scattered the proud in the imagination of their hearts.

He has brought down the mighty from their thrones,
and has exalted the humble and meek.

He has filled the hungry with good things,
and the rich he has sent empty away.

He, remembering his mercy,
has helped his servant Israel,

As he promised to our fathers,
Abraham and his seed for ever.

† Glory be to the Father, and to the Son, and to the Holy Spirit;
As it was in the beginning, is now, and ever shall be;
World without end. Amen.

The Creed

I believe in one God,
    the Father, the Almighty,
    maker of heaven and earth,
    of all that is, visible and invisible.

I believe in one Lord, Jesus Christ,
    the only-begotten Son of God,
    eternally begotten of the Father,
    God from God, Light from Light,
    true God from true God,
    begotten, not made,
    of one Being with the Father;
    through him all things were made.
For us and for our salvation he came down from heaven,
    was incarnate from the Holy Spirit and the Virgin Mary,
    and was made man.
For our sake he was crucified under Pontius Pilate;
    he suffered death and was buried.
On the third day he rose again in accordance with the Scriptures;
    he ascended into heaven
    and is seated at the right hand of the Father.
He will come again in glory to judge the living and the dead,
    and his kingdom will have no end.

I believe in the Holy Spirit, the Lord, the giver of life,
    who proceeds from the Father,
    who with the Father and the Son is worshiped and glorified,
    who has spoken through the prophets.
I believe in one holy catholic and apostolic Church.
I acknowledge one Baptism for the forgiveness of sins.
I look for the resurrection of the dead,
    † and the life of the world to come. Amen.

Officiant   Lord have mercy (upon us).

All   **Christ have mercy.**
Lord have mercy.

Our Father, who art in heaven,
hallowed be thy Name,
thy kingdom come,
thy will be done,
on earth as it is in heaven.
Give us this day our daily bread.
And forgive us our trespasses,
as we forgive those
who trespass against us.
And lead us not into temptation,
but deliver us from evil.
For thine is the kingdom,
and the power, and the glory,
for ever and ever. Amen.

Officiant   For the day that is past; that worry and every anxious fear
may be put away from us; and that Christ would be
glorified in all we have done, we pray to you O Lord.

All   **Lord, have mercy.**

Officiant   That this evening may be holy, good, and peaceful; that
the angels of the Lord our God would encamp around us;
and that our weary souls may find their rest in Christ our
Savior, we pray to you O Lord.

All   **Lord, have mercy.**

Officiant	Create in us clean hearts, O God;
All	**And renew a right spirit within us.**
Officiant	Grant us your peace;
All	**For only in you can we live in safety.**
Officiant	We pray for those in sickness, grief, persecution, bondage, fear, and loneliness.
All	**Lord, have mercy.**
Officiant	Let us offer our own prayers.

(pause to offer your own prayers or to sit in silence)

Collects
The Collect for the week may be said. Then,

Collect for Fridays

Lord Jesus Christ, by your death you took away the sting of death: Grant to us your servants so to follow in faith where you have led the way, that we may at length fall asleep peacefully in you and wake up in your likeness; for your tender mercies' sake. *Amen.*

Prayer for Mission

O God, you manifest in your servants the signs of your presence: Send forth upon us the Spirit of love, that in companionship with one another your abounding grace may increase among us; through Jesus Christ our Lord. *Amen.*

General Thanksgiving (said together)

Almighty God, Father of all mercies,
we your unworthy servants give you humble thanks
for all your goodness and loving-kindness
to us and to all whom you have made.
We bless you for our creation, preservation,
and all the blessings of this life;
but above all for your immeasurable love
in the redemption of the world by our Lord Jesus Christ;
for the means of grace, and for the hope of glory.
And, we pray, give us such an awareness of your mercies,
that with truly thankful hearts
we may show forth your praise,
not only with our lips, but in our lives,
by giving up our selves to your service,
and by walking before you
in holiness and righteousness all our days;
through Jesus Christ our Lord,
to whom, with you and the Holy Spirit,
be honor and glory throughout all ages. Amen.

Officiant   Let us bless the Lord.

All   **Thanks be to God.**

Officiant   † The grace of our Lord Jesus Christ, and the love of
God, and the fellowship of the Holy Spirit, be with us all
evermore. Amen.
2 Corinthians 13:14

Saturday
Evening Prayer

Officiant   † O God, make speed to save us.

All   **O Lord, make haste to help us.**

† Glory be to the Father, and to the Son, and to the Holy Spirit: as it was in the beginning, is now, and ever shall be, world without end. Amen.

Phos Hilaron
O Gladsome Light

O gladsome light of the holy glory
of the everliving Father in heaven,
O Jesus Christ, holy and blessed!

Now as we come to the setting of the sun,
and our eyes behold the vesper light,
we sing your praises, O God: Father, Son, and Holy Spirit.

You are worthy at all times to be praised by joyful voices,
O Son of God, Giver of Life,
and to be glorified through all the worlds.

A Psalm Appointed for Saturdays
The following or some other psalm may be said.

Psalm 27

The LORD is my light and my salvation;
whom shall I fear?

The LORD is the stronghold of my life;
of whom shall I be afraid?

When evildoers advance against me
to eat up my flesh,

my adversaries and my foes,
it is they who stumble and fall.

Though an army encamp against me,
my heart shall not fear;

Though war should arise against me,
even then I will be confident.

One thing I have asked of the LORD,
that will I seek after:

That I may dwell in the house of the LORD
all the days of my life,

to behold the beauty of the LORD
and to seek him in his temple.

For in the day of trouble he will hide me in his shelter;
he will conceal me in the cover of his tent;
he will set me high upon a rock.

And now my head shall be lifted up
above my enemies all around me,

And I will offer in his tent sacrifices of shouts of joy;
I will sing and make music to the LORD.

Hear my voice, O LORD, when I cry aloud;
have mercy on me and answer me!

You have said, "Seek my face."
My heart says to you,
"Your face, LORD, I will seek."

Hide not your face from me,
nor turn your servant away in anger.

You have been my help;
do not abandon me nor forsake me
O God of my salvation!

Though my father and my mother forsake me,
the LORD will take me in.

Teach me your way, O LORD,
and lead me on a level path
because of my enemies.

Deliver me not into the will of my adversaries;
for false witnesses have risen against me;
they breathe out violence.

I believe that I shall see the goodness of the LORD
in the land of the living!

Wait for the LORD;
be strong and let your heart take courage;
wait for the LORD!

At the end of the Psalms is said
† Glory be to the Father, and to the Son, and to the Holy Spirit:
as it was in the beginning, is now, and ever shall be,
world without end. Amen.

The Lessons

One or two Lessons from Scripture may be read. The following Canticle may be sung or said between or after the Lessons.

Magnificat
The Song of Mary - Luke 1:46-55

My soul magnifies the Lord,
and my spirit rejoices in God my Savior;

For he has regarded
the lowliness of his handmaiden.

For behold, from now on,
all generations will call me blessed;

For he that is mighty has magnified me,
and holy is his Name.

His mercy is on those who fear him,
throughout all generations.

He has shown the strength of his arm;
he has scattered the proud in the imagination of their hearts.

He has brought down the mighty from their thrones,
and has exalted the humble and meek.

He has filled the hungry with good things,
and the rich he has sent empty away.

He, remembering his mercy,
has helped his servant Israel,

As he promised to our fathers,
Abraham and his seed for ever.

† Glory be to the Father, and to the Son, and to the Holy Spirit;
As it was in the beginning, is now, and ever shall be;
World without end. Amen.

The Creed

I believe in one God,
>   the Father, the Almighty,
>   maker of heaven and earth,
>   of all that is, visible and invisible.

I believe in one Lord, Jesus Christ,
>   the only-begotten Son of God,
>   eternally begotten of the Father,
>   God from God, Light from Light,
>   true God from true God,
>   begotten, not made,
>   of one Being with the Father;
>   through him all things were made.

For us and for our salvation he came down from heaven,
>   was incarnate from the Holy Spirit and the Virgin Mary,
>   and was made man.

For our sake he was crucified under Pontius Pilate;
>   he suffered death and was buried.

On the third day he rose again in accordance with the Scriptures;
>   he ascended into heaven
>   and is seated at the right hand of the Father.

He will come again in glory to judge the living and the dead,
>   and his kingdom will have no end.

I believe in the Holy Spirit, the Lord, the giver of life,
>   who proceeds from the Father,
>   who with the Father and the Son is worshiped and glorified,
>   who has spoken through the prophets.

I believe in one holy catholic and apostolic Church.

I acknowledge one Baptism for the forgiveness of sins.

I look for the resurrection of the dead,
>   † and the life of the world to come. Amen.

Officiant   Lord have mercy (upon us).

All   **Christ have mercy.**
Lord have mercy.

Our Father, who art in heaven,
hallowed be thy Name,
thy kingdom come,
thy will be done,
on earth as it is in heaven.
Give us this day our daily bread.
And forgive us our trespasses,
as we forgive those
who trespass against us.
And lead us not into temptation,
but deliver us from evil.
For thine is the kingdom,
and the power, and the glory,
for ever and ever. Amen.

Officiant   For the day that is past; that worry and every anxious fear
may be put away from us; and that Christ would be
glorified in all we have done, we pray to you O Lord.

All   **Lord, have mercy.**

Officiant   That this evening may be holy, good, and peaceful; that
the angels of the Lord our God would encamp around us;
and that our weary souls may find their rest in Christ our
Savior, we pray to you O Lord.

All   **Lord, have mercy.**

Officiant	Create in us clean hearts, O God;
All	**And renew a right spirit within us.**
Officiant	Grant us your peace;
All	**For only in you can we live in safety.**
Officiant	We pray for those in sickness, grief, persecution, bondage, fear, and loneliness.
All	**Lord, have mercy.**
Officiant	Let us offer our own prayers.

(pause to offer your own prayers or to sit in silence)

Collects
The Collect for the week may be said. Then,

Collect for Saturdays

O God, the source of eternal light: Shed forth your unending day upon us who watch for you, that our lips may praise you, our lives may bless you, and our worship on the morrow give you glory; through Jesus Christ our Lord. *Amen.*

Prayer for Mission

O God and Father of all, whom the whole heavens adore: Let the whole earth also worship you, all nations obey you, all tongues confess and bless you, and men and women everywhere love you and serve you in peace; through Jesus Christ our Lord. *Amen.*

General Thanksgiving (said together)

Almighty God, Father of all mercies,
we your unworthy servants give you humble thanks
for all your goodness and loving-kindness
to us and to all whom you have made.
We bless you for our creation, preservation,
and all the blessings of this life;
but above all for your immeasurable love
in the redemption of the world by our Lord Jesus Christ;
for the means of grace, and for the hope of glory.
And, we pray, give us such an awareness of your mercies,
that with truly thankful hearts
we may show forth your praise,
not only with our lips, but in our lives,
by giving up our selves to your service,
and by walking before you
in holiness and righteousness all our days;
through Jesus Christ our Lord,
to whom, with you and the Holy Spirit,
be honor and glory throughout all ages. Amen.

Officiant   Let us bless the Lord.

All   **Thanks be to God.**

Officiant   † The grace of our Lord Jesus Christ, and the love of
                   God, and the fellowship of the Holy Spirit, be with us all
                   evermore. Amen.
                   2 Corinthians 13:14

COMPLINE

Compline

The Officiant begins
The Lord Almighty grant us a peaceful night and a perfect end. *Amen.*

Officiant	Our help is in the Name of the Lord;

All **The maker of heaven and earth.**

Officiant Let us humbly confess our sins to Almighty God.

All **Most merciful God,**
we confess that we have sinned against you
in thought, word, and deed,
by what we have done,
and by what we have left undone.
We have not loved you with our whole heart;
we have not loved our neighbors as ourselves.
We are truly sorry and we humbly repent.
For the sake of your Son Jesus Christ,
have mercy on us and forgive us;
that we may delight in your will,
and walk in your ways,
to the glory of your Name. Amen.

Officiant Almighty Father, who for your great love of your creation
did give your dearly beloved Son to die for us; Grant that
through his Cross † our sins may be put away, and
remembered no more against us, and that, cleansed by his
Blood, and mindful of his sufferings, we may take up our
cross daily, and follow him in newness of life, until we
come to his everlasting kingdom; through the Name of
your Son Jesus Christ our Lord. Amen.

Officiant   † O God, make speed to save us;

All   **O Lord, make haste to help us.**

† Glory be to the Father, and to the Son, and to the Holy Spirit: as it was in the beginning, is now, and ever shall be, world without end. Amen.

One or more of the following Psalms shall be said

Psalm 4

Hear me when I call, O God of my righteousness!
You have relieved me in my distress;
have mercy on me and hear my prayer.

O children of men, how long shall my glory be turned into shame?
How long will you love worthlessness and seek after lies?

Know that the LORD has set apart the godly for himself;
the LORD will hear when I call to him.

Be angry, and do not sin;
search your own hearts on your bed and be still.

Offer the sacrifices of righteousness,
and put your trust in the LORD.

There are many who say, "Who will show us some good?"
let the light of your face shine upon us, O LORD.

You have filled my heart with greater joy
than when their grain and wine abound.

I will lay me down and sleep in peace;
for you alone, O LORD, make me to dwell in safety.

Psalm 91

He who dwells in the shelter of the Most High
shall abide in the shadow of Shaddai.

He will say of the LORD, "He is my refuge and my fortress,
my God, in whom I trust."

Surely he will deliver you
from the snare of the fowler and from the deadly pestilence.

He will cover you with his feathers,
and under his wings you will find refuge;
his faithfulness is your shield and buckler.

You need not fear any terror of the night,
nor the arrow that flies by day,

Nor the pestilence that stalks in darkness,
nor the destruction that lays waste at noonday.

A thousand may fall at your side,
ten thousand at your right hand,
but it will not come near you.

You will only look on with your eyes
and see the recompense of the wicked.

Because you have made the LORD your refuge—
the Most High your habitation—

No evil shall be allowed to befall you,
nor any plague come near your tent.

For he will command his angels concerning you
to guard you in all your ways.

In their hands they will bear you up,
lest you dash your foot against a stone.

You will tread upon the lion and the adder;
the young lion and the serpent you will trample underfoot.

"Because he has loved me, therefore will I deliver him;
I will protect him, because he knows my Name.

When he calls upon me, I will answer him;
I will be with him in trouble;

I will deliver him and honor him.
With long life will I satisfy him
and show him my salvation."

Psalm 134

Behold, bless the LORD, all you servants of the LORD,
who stand by night in the house of the LORD!

Lift up your hands in the sanctuary,
and bless the LORD.

May the LORD bless you from Zion;
he who made heaven and earth.

At the end of the Psalms is said
✝ Glory be to the Father, and to the Son, and to the Holy Spirit:
as it was in the beginning, is now, and ever shall be,
world without end. Amen.

The following Scriptures are to be read on the appropriate day

———————

On Sundays

Lord, you are in the midst of us, and we are called by your Name: Do not forsake us, O Lord our God. *Jeremiah 14:9, 22*

A brief silence should be kept between readings.

Jesus said, "Do not be anxious, saying, 'What shall we eat?' or 'What shall we drink?' or 'What shall we wear?' For the pagans seek after all these things, and your heavenly Father knows that you need them all. But seek first the kingdom of God and his righteousness, and all these things will be added to you. Therefore do not be anxious about tomorrow, for tomorrow will be anxious for itself. Sufficient for the day is its own trouble." *Matthew 6:31-34*

On Mondays

May the God of peace who brought again from the dead our Lord Jesus, the great shepherd of the sheep, by the blood of the eternal covenant, equip you with everything good that you may do his will, working in you that which is pleasing in his sight, through Jesus Christ, to whom be glory for ever and ever. *Hebrews 13:20-21*

A brief silence should be kept between readings.

For if while we were enemies we were reconciled to God through the death of his Son, how much more, now that we are reconciled, shall we be saved by his life. More than that, we also rejoice in God through our Lord Jesus Christ, through whom we have now received reconciliation. *Romans 5:10-11*

On Tuesdays

Sing, O daughter of Zion! Shout, O Israel! Be glad and rejoice with all your heart, the LORD has taken away the judgments against you; he has cast out your enemy. The King of Israel, the LORD, is in your midst; you shall never again fear evil. The LORD your God is with you, a mighty warrior who will save. He will take great delight in you; He will quiet you with His love; He will rejoice over you with singing. *Zephaniah 3:14, 15, 17*

A brief silence should be kept between readings.

Jesus said, "I have said these things to you, that in me you may have peace. In the world you will have tribulation. But take heart; I have overcome the world." *John 16:33 ESV*

On Wednesdays

Jesus lifted up his eyes to heaven, and said, "Father, the hour has come; glorify your Son that the Son may glorify you, since you have given him authority over all flesh, to give eternal life to all whom you have given him. And this is eternal life, that they know you the only true God, and Jesus Christ whom you have sent." *John 17:1-3*

A brief silence should be kept between readings.

Jesus said to them, "Those who are healthy have no need of a physician, but those who are sick. Go and learn what this means: 'I desire mercy and not sacrifice.' For I did not come to call the righteous, but sinners."
Matthew 9:12-13

On Thursdays

Through Jesus Christ we have obtained access by faith into this grace in which we stand, and we rejoice in hope of the glory of God. Not only that, but we rejoice in our sufferings, knowing that suffering produces endurance, and endurance produces character, and character produces hope, and hope does not put us to shame, because God's love has been poured into our hearts through the Holy Spirit who has been given to us.
Romans 5:2-5 ESV

A brief silence should be kept between readings.

Jesus said, "O righteous Father, even though the world does not know you, I know you, and these know that you have sent me. I have made your Name known to them, and I will continue to make it known, so that the love with which you have loved me may be in them, and I in them."
John 17:25-26

On Fridays

For all who are led by the Spirit of God are children of God. For you did not receive a spirit of bondage again to fear, but you received the Spirit of adoption by whom we cry out, "Abba, Father." The Spirit himself bears witness with our spirit that we are children of God, and if children, then heirs—heirs of God and fellow heirs with Christ, provided we suffer with him in order that we may also be glorified with him."   *Romans 8:14-17*

A brief silence should be kept between readings.

Jesus said, "Come to me, all who labor and are heavy laden, and I will give you rest. Take my yoke upon you, and learn from me; for I am gentle and lowly in heart, and you will find rest for your souls. For my yoke is easy, and my burden is light."   *Matthew 11:28-30*

<u>On Saturdays</u>

Thus says the LORD, he who created you, O Jacob, he who formed you, O Israel: "Fear not, for I have redeemed you; I have called you by name, you are mine. When you pass through the waters, I will be with you; and through the rivers, they will not sweep over you; when you walk through fire you shall not be burned, the flame shall not consume you. For I am the LORD your God, the Holy One of Israel, your Savior."   *Isaiah 43:1-3*

A brief silence should be kept between readings.

Jesus said, "Which one of you, if his son asks him for bread, will give him a stone? Or if he asks for a fish, will give him a serpent? If you then, who are evil, know how to give good gifts to your children, how much more will your Father who is in heaven give good things to those who ask him! So whatever you wish that others would do to you, do also to them, for this is the Law and the Prophets."
Matthew 7:9-12 ESV

———————

A moment of silence should be kept after the readings. A suitable hymn may be sung.

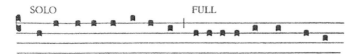

Be-fore the en-ding of the day, Cre-a-tor of the world, we pray

That with Thy won-ted fa-vor thou   Wouldst be our Guard and Keep-er now.

From all ill dreams de-fend our eyes, From night-ly fears and fan-ta-sies;

Tread un-der foot our ghost-ly foe, That no pol-lu-tion we may know.

O Fa-ther, that we ask be done, Through Je-sus Christ, thine on-ly Son;

Who, with the Ho-ly Ghost and thee, Doth live and reign e-ter-nal-ly.   A - men.

The Prayers

Officiant	Into your hands, O Lord, I commit my spirit.
All	**For you have redeemed me, O Lord, O God of truth.**
Officiant	Keep me as the apple of your eye.
All	**Hide me in the shadow of your wings.**

Officiant	Lord have mercy.
All	**Christ have mercy.** **Lord have mercy.**

All	**Our Father, who art in heaven,** **hallowed be thy Name,** **thy kingdom come, thy will be done,** **on earth as it is in heaven.** **Give us this day our daily bread.** **And forgive us our trespasses,** **as we forgive those who trespass against us.** **And lead us not into temptation,** **but deliver us from evil.** **For thine is the kingdom, and the power,** **and the glory, for ever and ever. Amen.**

Officiant	O Lord, hear our prayer;
All	**And let our cry come to you.**

The Officiant prays one or more of the following prayers.

O LORD, who has pity for all our weakness: Put away from us worry and every anxious fear, that, having ended the labors of the day, and committing our tasks, ourselves, and all we love into your keeping, we may, now that night is coming, receive from you your priceless gift of sleep; through Jesus Christ our Lord. *Amen.*

Be our light in the darkness, O Lord, and in your great mercy defend us from all perils and dangers of this night; for the love of your only Son, our Savior Jesus Christ. *Amen.*

Be present, O merciful God, and protect us through the hours of the night, so that we who are wearied by the changes and chances of this life may rest in your eternal changelessness; through Jesus Christ our Lord. *Amen.*

Visit this place, O Lord, and drive far from it all snares of the enemy; let your holy angels dwell with us to preserve us in peace; and let your blessing be upon us always; through Jesus Christ our Lord. *Amen.*

Silence is kept to offer personal prayers.

Conclusion & Blessing

Then the Officiant continues saying
Guide us waking, O Lord, and guard us sleeping, that awake we may watch with Christ, and asleep we may rest in peace.

Everyone:
Lord, now let your servant depart in peace,
according to your word.

For my eyes have seen your salvation,
which you have prepared before the face of all people;

To be a light to lighten the Gentiles,
and to be the glory of your people Israel.

† Glory be to the Father, and to the Son, and to the Holy Spirit;
As it was in the beginning, is now, and ever shall be;
World without end. Amen.

Everyone concludes with

Guide us waking, O Lord, and guard us sleeping, that awake we may
watch with Christ, and asleep we may rest in peace. Amen.

The Officiant concludes

The Almighty and Merciful Lord grant us a quiet night, and at the last a
perfect end; and the blessing of God Almighty, the Father, the Son, and
the Holy Spirit, be upon us and remain with us this night, and for
evermore. *Amen.*

BRIEF
RECOLLECTIONS

MORNING

† Lord, open my lips.
And my mouth shall proclaim your praise.

† O God, make speed to save me
O Lord, make haste to help me

† Glory be to the Father, and to the Son, and to the Holy Spirit; as it was in the beginning, is now, and ever shall be; world without end. Amen.

One or both of the following Psalms, or some other Psalm may be said

Psalm 3:1-5
O LORD, how many are my foes!
How many there are who rise up against me!
How many there are who say of my soul,
"There is no help for him in his God."
But you, O LORD, are a shield around me;
my glory, and the lifter of my head.
I cry aloud to the LORD,
and he answers me from his holy hill.
I lay me down and sleep;
I wake again, for the LORD sustains me.

Psalm 5:1-3
Give ear to my words, O LORD;
consider my sighing.
Give heed to the voice of my cry, my King and my God,
for to you do I pray.
In the morning, LORD, you hear my voice;
in the morning I will lay my requests before you
and eagerly wait.

A short selection of Scripture may be read followed by a brief silence.

The Creed may be said. Then,

Lord have mercy.
Christ have mercy.
Lord have mercy.

Our Father, who art in heaven,
hallowed be thy Name,
thy kingdom come, thy will be done,
on earth as it is in heaven.
Give us this day our daily bread.
And forgive us our trespasses,
as we forgive those who trespass against us.
And lead us not into temptation,
but deliver us from evil.
For thine is the kingdom, and the power,
and the glory, for ever and ever. Amen.

Final Collect
O God, the King eternal, whose light divides the day from the night and
turns the shadow of death into the morning: Drive far from us all wrong
desires, incline our hearts to keep your law, and guide our feet into the
way of peace; that, having done your will with cheerfulness during the
day, we may, when night comes, rejoice to give you thanks; through Jesus
Christ our Lord. *Amen.*

Final Blessing
† The grace of our Lord Jesus Christ, and the love of God, and the
fellowship of the Holy Spirit, be with us all evermore. Amen.
2 Corinthians 13:14

MID-DAY

† O God, make speed to save me
O Lord, make haste to help me

† Glory be to the Father, and to the Son, and to the Holy Spirit; as it was in the beginning, is now, and ever shall be; world without end. Amen.

One or more of the following, or some other Psalm may be said

Psalm 34:1-2
I will bless the LORD at all times;
his praise shall ever be in my mouth.
My soul shall make its boast in the LORD;
let the humble hear of it and rejoice.

Psalm 34:12-14
Who among you loves life
and desires long days, that he may see good?
Keep your tongue from evil
and your lips from speaking deceit.
Turn away from evil and do good;
seek peace and pursue it.

Psalm 34:17-18
The righteous cry and the LORD hears them;
he delivers them out of all their troubles.
The LORD is near to the brokenhearted
and saves those who are crushed in spirit.

A brief silence is kept. Then,

Lord have mercy.
Christ have mercy.
Lord have mercy.

Our Father, who art in heaven,
hallowed be thy Name,
thy kingdom come, thy will be done,
on earth as it is in heaven.
Give us this day our daily bread.
And forgive us our trespasses,
as we forgive those who trespass against us.
And lead us not into temptation,
but deliver us from evil.
For thine is the kingdom, and the power,
and the glory, for ever and ever. Amen.

Final Collect

Heavenly Father, send your Holy Spirit into our hearts, to direct and rule
us according to your will, to comfort us in all our afflictions, to defend us
from all error, and to lead us into all truth; through Jesus Christ our Lord.
Amen.

Final Blessing

† The grace of our Lord Jesus Christ, and the love of God, and the
fellowship of the Holy Spirit, be with us all evermore. Amen.
2 Corinthians 13:14

EVENING

† O God, make speed to save me
O Lord, make haste to help me

† Glory be to the Father, and to the Son, and to the Holy Spirit; as it was
in the beginning, is now, and ever shall be; world without end. Amen.

One or more of the following, or some other Psalm may be said

Psalm 19:1-4
The heavens declare the glory of God, *
and the skies proclaim the work of his hands.
Day unto day pours forth speech, *
and night unto night reveals knowledge.
There is no speech or language where their voice is not heard. *
Their voice goes out through all the earth,
and their words to the ends of the world.

Psalm 36:6-9
O LORD, you preserve both man and beast.
How precious is your steadfast love, O God!
The children of man take refuge in the shadow of your wings.
They feast on the abundance of your house;
you give them drink from the river of your delights.
For with you is the fountain of life;
in your light we see light.

Psalm 27:4
One thing I have asked of the LORD,
that will I seek after:
That I may dwell in the house of the LORD
all the days of my life,
to behold the beauty of the LORD
and to seek him in his temple.

A brief silence is kept. Then,

Lord have mercy.
Christ have mercy.
Lord have mercy.

Our Father, who art in heaven,
hallowed be thy Name,
thy kingdom come, thy will be done,
on earth as it is in heaven.
Give us this day our daily bread.
And forgive us our trespasses,
as we forgive those who trespass against us.
And lead us not into temptation,
but deliver us from evil.
For thine is the kingdom, and the power,
and the glory, for ever and ever. Amen.

Final Collect

Lord Jesus, stay with us, for evening is at hand and the day is past; be our companion in the way, kindle our hearts, and awaken hope, that we may know you as you are revealed in Scripture and the breaking of bread. Grant this for the sake of your love. *Amen.*

Final Blessing

† The grace of our Lord Jesus Christ, and the love of God, and the fellowship of the Holy Spirit, be with us all evermore. Amen.
2 Corinthians 13:14

AT BEDTIME

† In the Name of the Father, and of the Son, and of the Holy Spirit. Amen.

I will lay me down and sleep in peace; for you alone, O LORD, make me to dwell in safety. Amen. †

-- *then* –

Guide us waking, O Lord, and guard us sleeping, that awake we may watch with Christ, and asleep we may rest in peace. Amen. †

-- *then* –

The Almighty and Merciful Lord grant us a quiet night, and at the last a perfect end; and the blessing of God Almighty, † the Father, the Son, and the Holy Spirit, be upon us and remain with us this night, and for evermore. Amen.

NOTE: With young children, the following may be added before or in place of the "I will lay me down" prayer from Psalm 4 in the above Bedtime Prayers

Now I lay me down to sleep. I pray the Lord my soul to keep. Your love be with me through the night and wake me with the morning light. Amen. †

A GENERAL STRUCTURE FOR FAMILY PRAYER

An Opening sentence of Scripture may be said.

† O God, make speed to save us.
O Lord, make haste to help us.

† **Glory be to the Father, and to the Son, and to the Holy Spirit; as it
was in the beginning, is now, and ever shall be; world without end.
Amen.**

One or more selections from the Psalms may be read or recited together.

One or more other Scripture selections may be read.

A song may be sung.

The Creed may be said.

A brief silence is kept. Then,

Lord have mercy.
Christ have mercy.
Lord have mercy.

Our Father, who art in heaven,
hallowed be thy Name,
thy kingdom come, thy will be done,
on earth as it is in heaven.
Give us this day our daily bread.
And forgive us our trespasses,
as we forgive those who trespass against us.
And lead us not into temptation,
but deliver us from evil.
For thine is the kingdom, and the power,
and the glory, for ever and ever. Amen.

Each member of the family may be given time to pray freely.

One or more collects, blessings, or other prayers may be said.

The General Thanksgiving may be said together.

One of the following or some other final blessing may be said:

† The grace of our Lord Jesus Christ, and the love of God, and the fellowship of the Holy Spirit, be with us all evermore. Amen.
2 Corinthians 13:14

> *- or –*

May the Lord bless us and keep us; may the Lord make his face shine upon us and be gracious to us; may the Lord turn his face toward us and give us his peace.

† Glory be to the Father, and to the Son, and to the Holy Spirit; as it was in the beginning, is now, and ever shall be; world without end. Amen.

A FORM FOR PRIVATE PRAYER

†Lord, open my lips
And my mouth shall proclaim your praise.
† O God, make speed to save me
O Lord, make haste to help me

† Glory be to the Father, and to the Son, and to the Holy Spirit; as it was
in the beginning, is now, and ever shall be; world without end. Amen.

Venite *O Come*
Psalm 95:1-8; 96:9,13

O come, let us sing to the Lord;
let us shout for joy to the Rock of our salvation.
Let us come before his presence with thanksgiving
and raise a loud shout to him with psalms.

For the Lord is a great God,
and a great King above all gods.
In his hand are the caverns of the earth,
and the heights of the hills are his also.

The sea is his, for he made it,
and his hands have molded the dry land.
O come, let us worship and bow down,
and kneel before the Lord our Maker.

For he is our God,
and we are the people of his pasture and the sheep of his hand.
Today, if you hear his voice,
Do not harden your heart, as in the rebellion.

O worship the Lord in the beauty of holiness;
let the whole earth stand in awe of him.
For he comes, for he comes to judge the earth
and with righteousness to judge the world
and the peoples in his faithfulness.

Psalms
One or more psalms may be read.

At the end of the Psalms is said
† Glory be to the Father, and to the Son, and to the Holy Spirit:
as it was in the beginning, is now, and ever shall be,
world without end. Amen.

Lessons
One or two lessons from Scripture are read.

Canticles
One or (usually) both of the following canticles are said.

Song of Zechariah
Benedictus Dominus Deus • Luke 1: 68-79

Blessed be the Lord, the God of Israel;
he has come to his people and set them free.

He has raised up for us a mighty savior,
born of the house of his servant David.

Through his holy prophets he promised of old,
that he would save us from our enemies,
from the hands of all who hate us.

He promised to show mercy to our fathers
and to remember his holy covenant.

This was the oath he swore to our father Abraham,
to set us free from the hands of our enemies,

Free to worship him without fear,
holy and righteous in his sight
all the days of our life.

You, my child, shall be called the prophet of the Most High,
for you will go before the Lord to prepare his way,

To give his people knowledge of salvation
by the forgiveness of their sins.

In the tender compassion of our God
the dawn from on high shall break upon us,

To shine on those who dwell in darkness
and the shadow of death,
and to guide our feet into the way of peace.

† Glory be to the Father, and to the Son, and to the Holy Spirit:
as it was in the beginning, is now, and ever shall be,
world without end. Amen.

A Song to the Lamb
Dignus es • Revelation 4:11; 5:9-10, 13

Splendor and honor and kingly power
are yours by right, O Lord our God,

For you created everything that is,
and by your will they were created and have their being;

And yours by right, O Lamb that was slain,
for with your blood you have redeemed for God,

From every family, language, people, and nation,
a kingdom of priests to serve our God.

And so, to him who sits upon the throne,
and to Christ the Lamb,

Be worship and praise, dominion and splendor,
for ever and for evermore.

The Creed

I believe in one God,
    the Father, the Almighty,
    maker of heaven and earth,
    of all that is, visible and invisible.

I believe in one Lord, Jesus Christ,
    the only-begotten Son of God,
    eternally begotten of the Father,
    God from God, Light from Light,
    true God from true God,
    begotten, not made,
    of one Being with the Father;
    through him all things were made.
For us and for our salvation he came down from heaven,
    was incarnate from the Holy Spirit and the Virgin Mary,
    and was made man.
For our sake he was crucified under Pontius Pilate;
    he suffered death and was buried.
On the third day he rose again in accordance with the Scriptures;
    he ascended into heaven
    and is seated at the right hand of the Father.
He will come again in glory to judge the living and the dead,
    and his kingdom will have no end.

I believe in the Holy Spirit, the Lord, the giver of life,
    who proceeds from the Father,
    who with the Father and the Son is worshiped and glorified,
    who has spoken through the prophets.
I believe in one holy catholic and apostolic Church.
I acknowledge one Baptism for the forgiveness of sins.
I look for the resurrection of the dead,
    † and the life of the world to come. Amen.

Lord have mercy.
Lord Jesus Christ, Son of God, have mercy on me.
Lord have mercy.

The Lord's Prayer

Our Father in heaven,
hallowed be your Name,
your kingdom come,
your will be done,
on earth as it is in heaven.
Give us this day our daily bread.
And forgive us our trespasses,
as we forgive those
who trespass against us.
And lead us not into temptation,
but deliver us from the evil one.
For yours is the kingdom,
and the power, and the glory,
for ever and ever. Amen.

Intercessions

God of all creation, full of love and abounding in mercy;
May the whole earth be filled with your glory.

Lord, bless and guide all ministers of your church;
Clothe them in righteousness and grant them wisdom.

Direct the leaders of our nation;
That they may act in accordance with your kingdom.

Enlarge our own hearts, O Lord,
To love the things that you love.

May we proclaim your light
In every place where there is darkness.

May we proclaim your Holy Name
In every aspect of our lives.

Create in us clean hearts, O God;
And renew a right spirit within us.

Grant us your peace;
For only in you can we live in safety.

We pray for those in sickness, grief, persecution, bondage, fear, and
loneliness;
Lord, have mercy.

(pause to offer your own prayers and then to sit in silence)

Collects
The following Collect and any other appropriate Collects may be said.

O God, the King eternal, whose light divides the day from the night and
turns the shadow of death into the morning: Drive far from me all wrong
desires, incline my heart to keep your law, and guide my feet into the way
of peace; that, having done your will with cheerfulness during the day, I
may, when night comes, rejoice to give you thanks; through Jesus Christ
our Lord. *Amen.*

General Thanksgiving

Almighty God, Father of all mercies,
I your unworthy servant give you humble thanks
for all your goodness and loving-kindness
to me and to all whom you have made.
I bless you for my creation, preservation,
and all the blessings of this life;
but above all for your immeasurable love
in the redemption of the world by our Lord Jesus Christ;
for the means of grace, and for the hope of glory.
And, I pray, give me such an awareness of your mercies,
that with truly thankful heart
I may show forth your praise,
not only with my lips, but in my life,
by giving up my self to your service,
and by walking before you
in holiness and righteousness all my days;
through Jesus Christ our Lord,
to whom, with you and the Holy Spirit,
be honor and glory throughout all ages. Amen.

Conclusion
Let me bless you Lord.
Thanks be to God.

† The grace of my Lord Jesus Christ, and the love of God, and the
fellowship of the Holy Spirit, be with us all evermore. Amen.
2 Corinthians 13:14

May the words of my †mouth and the †meditation of my †heart be
pleasing in your sight, O Lord, my rock and my redeemer.

In the Name of the †Father, and of the Son, and of the Holy Spirit, I go
into this day.

Glory to you Lord Jesus Christ. Glory forever.

Printed in Great Britain
by Amazon

81819475R00129